# SACRED STORY

Teacher Resource Guide

Seventh Grade

"Creation, Presence, Memory & Mercy"

Sacred Story Press
1401 E Jefferson St, STE 405
Seattle, WA 981222

Copyright © 2016

All rights reserved. No part of this book shall be reproduced, stored in a retrieval system, or transmitted by any means – electronic, mechanical, photocopying, recording, or otherwise – without written permission from the publisher. The only exception is brief quotations in printed reviews. Although every precaution has been taken in the preparation of this book, the publisher and author assume no responsibility for errors or omissions. Neither is any liability assumed for damages resulting from the use of the information contained herein.

**Dedicated to Our Lady of the Way**

ISBN-13: 978-1533611284
ISBN-10: 1533611289

Unless otherwise indicated, Scripture quotations are from the Holy Bible, *New American Bible, revised edition* © 2010, 1991, 1986, 1970 Confraternity of Christian Doctrine, Washington, D.C.

Cover Art by Léopold Marboeuf
Used with Permission: Templegate Publishers
Jacket and Book Design: William Watson, SJ

# Table of Contents

About Sacred Story Youth.................................................................1

Program Overview ......................................................................5

Sacred Story Youth in Four Steps..................................9

Information Letter for Parents.......................................10

Teacher Unit Plan Overview .........................................12

Lesson One.......................................................................21

Lesson Two......................................................................32

Lesson Three...................................................................43

Certificate of Appreciation ............................................50

Teacher Theological Resource Guide ..........................51

Forward Inspirations – Children in Scripture...............................................52

Modern Missions to the Society of Jesus and Goals from Recent General Congregations...53

Inspirations from Recent Popes and Councils on Evangelization..........................56

Introduction..................................................................................62

Chapter One: A Simple Catechesis on Creation and the Fall..................................64

Chapter Two: God Calls Us to Come Home for the Joy of Reconciliation....................83

Chapter Three: A Short Course on Spiritual Discernment..................................93

Chapter Four: The Ten Commandments – God's Relational Codes............................113

## About Sacred Story Youth

Over two years in development and tested with hundreds of students and teachers, Sacred Story Youth (SSY) is a new prayer program designed to teach the classic Ignatian Examination of Conscience in a new way to children in Pre-K to Eight Grade. It is intended for use by teachers, parents, youth ministers and anyone else who is interested in helping youth learn how to pray and understand spiritual discernment. The five movements of the Sacred Story Prayer (Creation, Presence, Memory, Mercy and Eternity) are combined with various Commandments at each grade level to help youth learn both the content of their faith as well how to connect with God personally in prayer.

The heart of the SSY program is a guided meditation created in twenty renditions for each grade level that students do daily. The recorded guided meditations use two musical settings from the #1 Billboard piano artist, Paul Cardall, and each music settings has five different nature settings (ocean, lake, forest, prairie and mountain) for listening/prayer variety.

## Sacred Story Cross

Sacred Story Institute (SSI) has also created Sacred Story Cross as a learning aid that is available in six colors from our SSI store (store.sacredstory.net) or purchased in bulk at lower prices (see below). It works for Pre-K through eighth grade and combines the Ten Commandments with the five letters for the five-movements of Sacred Story Prayer (C-Creation; P-Presence; M-Memory; M-Mercy; E-Eternity). The Sacred Story Cross is a tactile learning aid that your students can use to complement the practice of Sacred Story Prayer's five movements (Creation, Presence, Memory, Mercy & Eternity) with the Ten Commandments that accompany each level. Sacred Story Cross works as a sacred object, a puzzle and a reminder to pray daily. Crosses can be purchased at store.sacredstory.net.

## Student Meditation Response Log Books

SSI also has available SSY Meditation Response Log Books that help students follow their daily spiritual growth. The Meditation Books with one year's worth of daily logs eliminate the need for copying the templates. Books can be ordered on AMAZON for $6.95 or in bulk from SSI for $4.00 each. If you want to order in bulk Meditation Response Logs or Sacred Story Cross from SSI, contact us at admin-team@sacredstory.net and let us know the number of books and crosses and which level(s) and colors.

The great benefit of the *Meditation Response Log Books* is that the daily jotting of one thing that makes one happy or sad (and in the upper grades, we use the Ignatian words consolation and desolation) is that it helps youth attune to the spiritual world. The jottings are not a diary but spiritual reflections that deal with things that "increase in faith, hope and love" or cause a decrease in those same three core elements of the spiritual life. See the sample responses in the back of the book for this important aspect of *Sacred Story Youth*. [i]

Occasionally students might reveal more serious issues in their lives and this can be a great benefit for helping the youth find the answers they need. The current national requirements of education law requires all teachers, <u>no matter the grade or subject content</u>, to report to the proper authorities (usually parents) if they are concerned about the emotional or physical well-being of a student. So no matter the subject or grade, teachers should peruse the papers, essays, homework assignments or response logs to ensure the lessons are being completed correctly, and to be alert to the occasional student whose homework assignment might indicate distress.

## Sacred Story Youth PDF Downloads and Power Points from sacredstory.net

Go to sacredstory.net and sign up to be a member. It is free! On the Member's Page you will find a category for Sacred Story Youth. All of the main documents/handouts and Power Points (most that are in this manual) are available in full color as PDF's. These include for each grade level.

**Sacred Story in Four Steps**

**Information Letter for Parents**

**Lessons One-Three**

**Scope and Sequence for Each Grade Level**

**Power Point Presentation on the Life of St. Ignatius Unique for Each Grade Level**

**Certificate of Appreciation**

### MP3 for Youth During Vacations and Summertime
The daily practice of keeping track of the spiritual movements of "consolation and desolation" (what makes me happy and what makes me sad) in the Meditation Response Logs is important for a child's awakening to the spiritual world.

To facilitate this, we have made all the meditation songs available as individual MP3's which are purchasable from store.sacredstory.net for just ninety-nine cents. Children can download their favorite and have it on their playback device of choice.

# THE HEART OF SACRED STORY YOUTH PROGRAM

Learn this and you will understand
the heart of Sacred Story Youth Program!

## THE RECORDED SACRED STORY DAILY PRAYER MEDITATION IS TO BE FREGULARLY, DAILY IF POSSIBLE!

## YET EACH DAY IT IS A DIFFERENT EXPERIENCE FOR YOUR STUDENTS!

## WHY? BECAUSE THEY BRING NEW PERSONAL EXPERIENCES TO THE EXAMEN PRAYER EACH DAY!

## TRUST THE ANCIENT WISDOM OF THE IGNATIAN DAILY EXAMEN!

## DON'T THINK THEY WILL GET BORED!

## A NOTE ON MEDITATION RESPONSE LEARNING LOGS!

It is the use of the Learning Logs that will provide the most helpful daily lesson for the students in keeping track of their spiritual movements. You, they, and their parents will begin to see the development in what students are learning as the meditation practice gains depth.

# Program Overview

You are about to embark on a relationship building journey with your students! This journey is one where children are provided the opportunity to attune themselves to listening to God's voice. *Sacred Story Youth* presents a model for mapping and connecting relationships between self and God and self and others. It is a sophisticated application of the time-tested Ignatian Examination of Conscience for children.

What is most important to this prayer discipline? It is the <u>daily repetition</u> of the guided meditation that will slowly draw children of all ages into their interior life where they will learn to "discern" the voice that leads to God and the voice that leads away from God.

The teaching of religious content, doctrines, commandments and sacraments is significantly enlivened when children have an *active* relationship with Christ and God. The *Sacred Story Youth* course is designed to augment regular religious training and so make faith come alive.

As an educator, you know that repetition is the key to learning. The listening and engagement of the "same" prayer meditation each and every day will not elicit the "same" response on the part of a student. While the meditation text/themes/music are similar daily, the spiritual, emotional, intellectual and physical nature of a person, made in God's image and likeness, is constantly changing. Like any regular prayer discipline, these meditations will strike a new cord each day and will gain depth as the children progress.

Why? Because the repetition of the guided meditation will be fresh each day as students' interior lives open to their spiritual nature. The body and mind constantly grow. This is even truer of our spiritual lives. *Sacred Story Youth* is designed to feed the interior spiritual life of children.

You can tell the students that they will be listening to the same words and music daily. Also tell them that because they are different day to day, God will respond differently to what is happening in their hearts and minds that particular day. So every day will actually be different! You can tell them that they will learn to listen deeply to their hearts and find the voice of God present thereto them daily in the very way they need God.

We are grateful that you using this new spiritual resource!

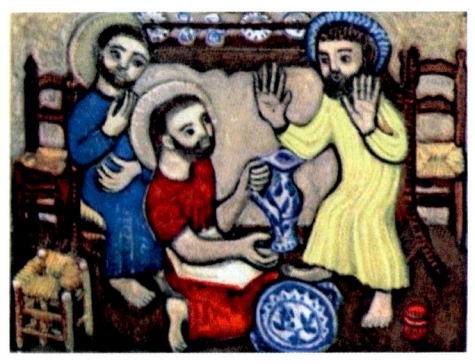

# Meditation Themes
# &
# Prayer Reflection Lyrics

*SACRED STORY* prayer has five meditation themes. As the students grow through the years they will experience each theme. Beginning in Pre-Kindergarten there is one theme per grade level.

Starting in fifth grade students start to do more than one theme a day until they reach all five per day in grade eight.

### CREATION
*Father, I believe You created everything out of love as a gift for me.*

### PRESENCE
*Father, I believe You are present in every moment and event of my life.*

### MEMORY
*Father, I believe Jesus helps me remember everything I have done or has been done to me that has hurt my life of*
*faith, hope and love.*

### MERCY
*Father, I believe that You showed us in Jesus that mercy and forgiveness is the greatest expression of Your love.*

### ETERNITY
*Father, I believe You can give me eternal love because by Jesus' passion, death, and resurrection you make*
*this Eternal Kingdom possible.*

# VIMEO LYRICS

## SEVENTH GRADE

### CREATION–PRESENCE–MEMORY–MERCY

*Introduction (1 Minute)*
*Jesus, help me slow down and hear You in my heart.*

*Middle Section*

*CREATION (1 Minute)*
*Father I believe You created everything out of love as a gift for me.*
*Jesus, as the music plays, I ask You to help me remember the gift in Your creation that brought me the most faith, hope and love today.*
*When You help me remember, I will thank You for that gift.*
*PRESENCE (1 Minute)*
*Father I believe You are present in every moment and event of my life. Jesus, I ask for a heart-felt knowledge of Your love for me.*
*Jesus, as the music plays, I ask You to help me know what my heart is feeling now. If I am peaceful, I will tell You why. If I am sad, I will tell You why.*

*MEMORY (1 Minute)*
*Father I believe Jesus helps me remember everything that I have done or that has been done to me that has hurt my life of faith, hope and love.*
*Jesus, As the music plays, I ask You to open my memory to these sinful things so that Your love can heal me.*

*MERCY (1 Minute)*
*Father I believe that You showed us in Jesus that mercy and forgiveness is the greatest expression of Your love.*
*Jesus, as the music plays, I will tell You the things I have done for which I need Your forgiveness and mercy. I will also tell You the things that others have done to me so I can offer Your mercy and forgiveness to them.*

***Closing (2 Minutes)***
*CREATION—PRESENCE—MEMORY—MERCY*
*Father, let me always be grateful for Your gift of life and I pray I serve only You, the true God of Life and Love.*

*Let me always know what leads to life and what leads to death.*
*I know You will always be with me.*
*Jesus, I pray with You to the Father in the words You taught us:*
*Our Father who art in heaven, hallowed be thy name.*

*Thy kingdom come, thy will be done, on earth, as it is in heaven. Give us this day our daily bread, and forgive us our trespasses, as we forgive those who trespass against us. And lead us not into temptation, but deliver us from evil. AMEN.*

As I return to my day, Jesus, let me always be grateful for my life.
As the music comes to an end, I ask in my own words for the grace to serve only You and Your Kingdom of Life and Light.

# SACRED STORY YOUTH
## IN FOUR EASY STEPS

**Teach Lesson One**

⇩

**Teach Lesson Two**

⇩

**Teach Lesson Three**

⇩

Listen to 3-8 minute Meditation Daily
Students Then Write a
One Minute Reflection Daily or Weekly

# Sacred Story Youth Information Letter for Parents

Dear Seventh Grader Parent/Guardian:

Sacred Story Institute (SSI) developed a new Ignatian Pre-K to grade 8 conscience formation program called Sacred Story Youth (SSY). SSY took two and a half years to develop and was tested with hundreds of students and teachers across six dioceses in the United States. The program is designed to use a three to five minute space after recess each day to teach the Ignatian "examination of conscience" in a new rendition called Sacred Story Prayer.

The program's main teaching tool is recorded guided meditations that are age appropriate for each of the Pre-K to 8 grades. The three-eight minute guided meditations are designed to be used to quiet the mind and guide students learn how to hear the voice of God in their hearts.

This is a yearlong meditative experience to help children build sensitivity and awareness of God's presence in their lives, to allow God to shape one's *Sacred Story* according to his will and graces. St Ignatius, the founder of the Jesuits (Society of Jesus) used the examination of conscience every day and teaches us that spiritual conversion is not a single event but a life-long process.

The seventh graders focus on the Sacred Story meditation themes of CREATION, PRESENCE, MEMORY & MERCY linked with the 1st Commandment (I Am The Lord Your God-You Shall Have No Strange Gods Before Me) with the reflection: **I believe God loved me into life and I commit to the relationship by giving all my mind, heart, and strength to God alone and will serve no other god.**

There are two storylines to this relational paradigm: I can choose to serve the Lord of Life and Light and help build His Kingdom by only cooperating with the forces of light or I can choose to serve the lord of darkness and death build his kingdom by cooperating with the forces of darkness--No one can serve two masters.

Sacred Story Youth uses a "relational paradigm" for understanding creation, the fall and redemption. Sacred Story's relational paradigm provides a new and intuitive way to understand the most complex and important dimension to the Story of the cosmos and human life. Pope Francis called the Creation a "love story" that to our day is still being written.

We invite you to visit store.sacredstory.net to see our work and hear a sample meditation for the children. If you have any questions, please contact your child's teacher.

Sincerely,

*Fr. Bill Watson, S.J.*
*President/Founder*

1401 E Jefferson
Suite 405
Seattle, WA 98122

# SACRED STORY YOUTH

## UNIT PLAN OVERVIEW
## SEVENTH GRADE LEVEL

# UNIT PLAN[1]

## Title/Theme:
*Sacred Story: An Ignatian Examen for the Third Millennium*

## Grade Seven/Religion

## Length of Unit/Timeframe:

There are three lessons to set purpose at beginning of year followed by daily 6-8 minute meditations.

## Description:

Ignatius' spirituality and discernment techniques rely on affective information to help individuals understand the difference between right and wrong. We can train people to listen deeply to their hearts—their consciences—to distinguish the ideas and inspirations coming from the Lord of Life and those Ignatius describes as coming from the enemy of human nature.

This is a yearlong meditative experience to help children build sensitivity and awareness of God's presence in their lives, to allow God to shape one's *Sacred Story* according to his will and graces. Ignatius' life-long examination indicates that conversion is not a single event but a life-long process. Ignatian spirituality helps one attune to the voice of God, the voice of the self and the voice of the "enemy of human nature". In attuning to these three distinct personal forces or voices, one can learn how to follow Divine inspiration in all life choices and relationships.

## Overview:

The relational paradigm in seventh grade is "My Relationship with Christ and His Kingdom of Truth and Light – serving Him alone". This relational paradigm is a model for mapping and connecting relationships between self and God as well as self and others.

*************************************************************

---

[1] Original template by Susan Abelein, Ph.D. Catapult Learning, LLC; this template created in consultation: Susan Abelein, Ph.D., Carole Eipers, Laura Egan, Mary Jane Krebbs, Ph.D., Lorraine A. Ozar, Ph.D., Leanne Welch, PBVM for the Common Core Catholic Identity Initiative (CCCII). June 2012

# THE BIG PICTURE

## Essential Question:

How do I listen to the voice of God, the voice of the self and the voice of the "enemy of human nature" so that I may follow Divine inspiration in all life choices and relationships?

## Storylines to this Relational Paradigm:

There are two storylines to this relational paradigm:

I can choose to serve the Lord of Life and Light and help build His Kingdom by only cooperating with the forces of light

*OR*

I can choose to serve the lord of darkness and death build his kingdom by cooperating with the forces of darkness--No one can serve two masters.

# CATHOLIC IDENTITY ELEMENTS

## CATECHISM OF THE CATHOLIC CHURCH REFERENCES

- Paragraph 2705 - II. Meditation
  2705 **Meditation** is above all a quest. The mind seeks to understand the why and how of the Christian life, in order to adhere ...
- Paragraph 2706 - II. Meditation
  ... To the extent that we are humble and faithful, we discover in **meditation** the movements that stir the heart and we are able to discern them. ...
- Paragraph 2708 - II. Meditation
  2708 **Meditation** engages thought, imagination, emotion, and desire. This mobilization of faculties is necessary in order ...
- Paragraph 2707 - II. Meditation
  2707 There are as many and varied methods of **meditation** as there are spiritual masters. Christians owe it to themselves ...
- Paragraph 2721 - III. Contemplative Prayer
  2721 The Christian tradition comprises three major expressions of the life of prayer: vocal prayer, **meditation**, and contemplative prayer. ...

- <u>Paragraph 2729 - II. Humble Vigilance of Heart</u>
  ... in vocal prayer; it can concern, more profoundly, him to whom we are praying, in vocal prayer (liturgical or personal), **meditation**, and contemplative ...
- Paragraph 295 - IV. The Mystery of Creation
  295 We believe that God created the world according to his wisdom. 141 It is not the product of any necessity whatever, nor of blind fate or chance
- Paragraph 239 - II. The Revelation of God as Trinity
  239 By calling **God** "Father," the language of faith indicates two main things: that **God** is the first origin of everything and transcendent authority; and he is at the same time goodness and loving care for all his children.
- Paragraph 1863 - IV. The Gravity of Sin: Mortal and Venial Sin
  1863 Venial **sin** weakens charity; it manifests a disordered affection for created goods; it impedes the soul's progress in the exercise of the virtues ..
- Paragraph 1857 - IV. The Gravity of Sin: Mortal and Venial Sin
  1857 For a **sin** to be mortal, three conditions must together be met: "Mortal **sin** is **sin** whose object is grave matter and which is also committed with ...
- Paragraph 1859 - IV. The Gravity of Sin: Mortal and Venial Sin
  1859 Mortal **sin** requires full knowledge and complete consent. It presupposes knowledge of the sinful character of the ...
- Paragraph 2092 - I. "You Shall Worship the Lord Your God and Him Only Shall You Serve" ... own capacities, (hoping to be able to save himself without help from on high), or he presumes upon **God's** almighty power or his **mercy** (hoping to ...
- Paragraph 1847 - I. Mercy and Sin
  1847 "**God** created us without us: but he did not will to save us without us." 116 To receive his **mercy**, we must admit our faults. ...

# Six Tasks of Catechesis & Essential Concepts

### TASK 3 – MORALITY/LIFE IN CHRIST
– Students develop a moral conscience that is informed by Church teachings and conformed to Christ, as modeled in a personal life of virtue and demonstrate in service of the Gospel's demands for society.

**M-HP. THE HUMAN PERSON [1700-1701]**
M-HP-1. Made in the Image of God- Foundation of Human Dignity
M-HP-3. Human Freedom and Conscience Formation [1730-1743, 1749-1794]
M-HP-4. Covenant and the Ten Commandments [2052-2074].

**E-HC THE HUMAN COMMUNITY**
M-HC.1. Personal and Social Sin [1846-1860].

### TASK 4 – PRAYER
**P-UC. THE UNIVERSAL CALL TO PRAYER, IMPORATANCE OF PRAYER [2566-2567]**
**P.EP. EXPRESSIONS OF PRAYER** – personal and shared, vocal, singing, meditation [2699-2719].

## LOCAL DIOCESE OR ARCHDIOCESAN STANDARDS

Many diocese and archdioceses are rewriting their catechetical standards based on new USCCB updates required of Catholic schools. Below is a sample of how the Sacred Story Youth Program matches the Seattle Archdiocese's Religion Standards updated in 2014 with the Six Tasks of Catechesis and Essential Concepts.

***Please send Sacred Story Institute your own diocesan or archdiocesan standards as we are creating a single document for all school systems that will list the local standards for the Sacred Story Youth program. Send these standards to: admin-team@sacredstory.net with the email title: "Religion Standards for (your dioceses' name)."***

- ❖ 7-ME-HP-1 Identify how we are created in God's image.

- 7-ME-HP-1 Identify how we are called to know God and proclaim the Good News of Jesus Christ by the way we live and act.
- 7-ME-HP-1 Explore ways of being models of Christian love in everyday life.
- 7-ME-HP-3 Locate New Testament passages that provide examples of Jesus helping to form the consciences of believers: Matthew 5.
- 7-ME-HP-4 Discuss how the Ten Commandments are a guide for moral living
- 7-ME-HC-1 State how personal sins have social consequences.
- 7-TP--UC Explain how prayer can help in times of temptation
- 7-TP-UC Discuss how prayer expresses their deepest needs, in times of temptation, and as an act of self-surrender to God. 7-TP-EP Explain how prayer expresses their relationship with God
- 7-TP-EP Recognize meditation as an important form of prayer.
- 7-TP-EP Participate in a variety of traditional devotions, and experience different prayer forms.

***********************************************************************

# Common Core
## Standards for English Language Arts

- L7.6 Acquire and use accurately grade-appropriate general academic and domain-specific words and phrases; gather vocabulary knowledge when considering a word or phrase important to comprehension or expression.
- SL7.1. Engage effectively in a range of collaborative discussions (one-on-one, in groups, and teacher-let) with diverse partners on grade 8 topics, texts, and issues, building on others' ideas and expressing their own clearly.
- W7.10 Write routinely over extended time frames (time for research, reflection and revision) and shorter time frames (a single sitting or a day or two) for a range of discipline-specific tasks, tasks purposes and audiences.

***********************************************************************

# KEY OBJECTIVES LINKED TO THE STANDARDS

- ❖ At the end of these lessons students will be begin to participate in Ignatian discernment and attentiveness in daily meditation exercises to deepen their relationship with God.
- ❖ The student can begin to discern God's voice in his/her life to reset his/her relationship with God, our source of life, who is love.
- ❖ The student will practice recording ideas in Learning Log .
- ❖ The student will be able to begin to discern God's voice in his/her life to reset his/her relationship with God, our source of life, who is love by fully participating in the meditation and reflection process.
  .

**Summative Assessment(s):** To reflect on what increased faith, hope and love and what diminished faith, hope and love. Students participate in daily meditation and reflecting in learning logs.

*******************************************************************************

# VOCABULARY

Tier 2 words: prayer
Tier 3 words: Meditation, Sacred Story, Creation, Presence, Memory, Mercy, Consolation, Desolation

## Text Resources for teacher:

- ❖ Watson, William M. *Sacred Story: An Ignatian Examen for the Third Millennium*. Seattle, WA: Sacred Story, 2012. Print.
- ❖ Bible
- ❖ Vimeo based Meditations for Sacred Story Youth. Music by Paul Cardall: www.paulcardall.com Copyright 2008 Used by Permission (BMI)

*******************************************************************************

# INSTRUCTIONAL ACTIVITIES

- ❖ Catholic Identity
- ❖ Speaking/Listening
- ❖ Vocabulary
- ❖ Critical Thinking
- ❖ Meditation
- ❖ Prayer

*****************************************************************************

# LESSON OVERVIEW

## Sacred Story Youth
## Consists of Three Introductory Lessons
## Followed by the Daily Meditation Practice

- ❖ Lesson One: Introduces the meditation step(s) focus for the grade level.

- ❖ Lesson Two: Introduces the "Right Relationship" based on the grades Commandment(s) focus for the year with a PowerPoint connecting St. Ignatius' life experiences to this commandment.

- ❖ Lesson Three: Combines the meditation step and "Right Relationship" to provide the set and practice for doing the meditation. The Learning Log is introduced in this lesson as well.

- ❖ Begin Daily Meditation: Once the three introductory lessons have been taught the daily meditations can begin. Access to the audio meditations is in Lesson Three.

*********************************************************************************

# HELPFUL HINTS

- **Teach the three lessons prior to beginning the daily meditations.**

- ***Please read each lesson*** prior to teaching as there are materials and internet access required in some of the lessons.

- A few lessons suggest getting supplies on your own (i.e. first and third grade).

- ***All lessons require access to internet***, speakers and a computer that can play from Vimeo for students to participate. **Please test your internet connections prior to teaching.**

- **The Audio Guided Prayer Meditations are the core of the Sacred Story Youth Program** and they range in length from just under three minutes to about eight minutes, depending on the grade/sophistication level of the students. It is our expectation that all grades may find the length long at first, but continued "practice" will help students find the interior quiet they both long for and need to be more peaceful people.

- ***Most lessons have "templates"*** or worksheet pages for teachers to copy for their students.

- **Lesson 3 post-reflection exercise is key to the audio meditations. "Learning Logs" are the core to the meditation reflections.** Teachers should copy the "Learning Logs" back to back. One copy is needed per week in grades one through eight.

**NOTE:** It is advised to copy the "Learning Logs" in monthly or quarterly packets for easy access. Or you can purchase from Amazon or Sacred Story Institute pre-prepared one-year **Meditation Response** books for this grade level. For bulk discounts contact us at admin-team@sacredstory.net

# LESSON ONE

**Objective: The students will be able to name and define the five meditation themes for *Sacred Story*, Creation, Presence, Memory, and Mercy, by explaining and listening with a jigsaw activity with 100% accuracy.**

- **Materials:**
  - PowerPoint of St. Ignatius Loyola's Story
  - Projector
  - Computer
  - Copies of definition for creation, presence, memory and mercy
  - Copies of response sheet for all students and copies of prayer sheet for all students
  - Students may need markers, crayons, pens or pencils

# LESSON ONE

**Invitation to Prayer:**

Gather class together in prayer corner

**Open with prayer:** The Creation Illuminative Prayer

*Here I ask for what I desire: to know and feel God's tender and passionate love and to know myself as beloved – a treasure of God's heart in the grand symphony of creation. I pray for the grace of gratitude. In particular, I pray to know by whom I am created and why I am loved. I pray to know and believe that I am fearfully and wonderfully made.*

**Introduction:** This school year we will be experiencing a meditation practice called *Sacred Story Youth*. *Sacred Story Youth* is inspired by St. Ignatius Loyola's "Examen". Ignatius' spirituality and discernment techniques rely on affective information to help individuals understand the difference between right and wrong. This year we will focus on "My Relationship with Christ and His Kingdom of Truth and Light – serving Him alone" which is inspired from the First Commandment: I am the Lord your God, you shall have no strange gods before me.

***Access PowerPoint to tell St. Ignatius Loyola's story to the students***

We can learn to listen deeply with our hearts—our consciences—to distinguish the ideas and inspirations coming from the Lord of Life and those Ignatius describes as coming from the enemy of human nature.

*Today we will be able to name and define the four meditation themes for Sacred Story: Creation, Presence, Memory, and Mercy, by identifying how you see God in your lie in each of the themes.*

Give each student copies of the four meditation themes and the Theme Template. Divide the class into small groups, preferably four groups.

**Guided Practice:**

(15 minutes) Divide students into four groups.  Have each group identify a leader, a timekeeper, a recorder, a reporter.

> The leader will keep the group's attention to the task at hand.
> The time keeper will assure the project is done in the time allotted.
> The recorder writes, draws or creates the notes from the group discussion
> The reporter will be the group representative to report back to the group.

## *Directions:*

1. Assign a theme to each group. Each group is to take 3-5 minutes to read the definition, Prelude, Illuminative Grace, and psalm for one of the themes.
2. The groups get 10 minutes to fill in their theme's section with examples of how they see God in their relationship.
3. These examples must be shared in 2-3 minutes.

## Whole Class Review: (10-15 minutes)

Each group shares their examples of the meditation theme assigned to their group. Consider posting these in the classroom near the prayer corner to reference when meditating. Students who are listening are to fill in the additional themes with ideas they hear from the group presentations.

## Independent Practice: (could be homework)

Then have each student write a personal prayer asking God to open everyone in the class to serving His Kingdom of light and to be protected from serving the forces of darkness.  Be specific in the prayer.

## Closure:

Each day we will be listening to a meditation and writing in our Learning Logs. Our thoughts will be centering on the four meditation steps:  Creation, Presence, Memory and Mercy.  Share with the students the following reflections they will be hearing on the MP3.

## CREATION
*Father I believe you created everything out of love as a gift for me.*
*I ask you Jesus to help me remember the gift in your creation that brought me the most faith, hope and love today.*
*When you help me remember, I will thank You for that gift.*

## PRESENCE
*Father I believe you are present in every moment and event of my life. I ask for a heart-felt knowledge of Jesus' love for me.*
*I ask you Jesus to help me know what my heart is feeling now.*
*If I am peaceful, I will tell You why. If I am sad, I will tell You why.*

## MEMORY
*Father I believe Jesus helps me remember everything that I have done or that has been done to me that has hurt my life of faith, hope and love.*
*I ask you Jesus to open my memory to these sinful things*
*so that your love can heal me.*

## MERCY
*Father I believe that you showed us in Jesus that mercy and forgiveness is the greatest expression of Your love.*
*I will tell you the things I have done for which I need Your forgiveness and mercy.*
*I will also tell you the things that others have done to me*
*so I can offer Your mercy and forgiveness to them.*

# CREATION

*I believe God created everything in love and for love; I ask for **heart-felt** knowledge of God's love **for me,** and for **gratitude** for the **general** and **particular graces** of **this day.***

### *Prelude*

*God created the universe – all person and all things – in love and for love. Every thing, and every person in creation is linked in Love, through Christ, in whom and for whom everything was made. We are made to reverence God and each other, and to delight in creation as both Divine gift and support for our lives. The God of All knows me personally and loves me, even before I was knit in my mother's womb. So fearfully and wonderfully made am I!*
(Ps 139:13-14)

### *Illuminative Grace*

*Here I ask for what I desire: to know and feel God's tender and passionate love and to know myself as beloved – a treasure of God's heart in the grand symphony of creation. I pray for the grace of gratitude. In particular, I pray to know by whom I am created and why I am loved. I pray to know and believe that I am fearfully and wonderfully made.*

When I see your heavens, the work of your fingers, The moon and stars that you set in place – What is man that you are mindful of him, And a son of man that you care for him? Yet you have made him little less than a god, Crowned him with glory and honor You have given him rule over the works of your hands, put all things at his feet: O LORD, our Lord, how awesome is your name through all the earth!
(Ps 8:4-6)

# PRESENCE

I believe God is **present** in **moment** and **event** of my life, and I ask for grace to **awaken, see** and **feel** where and how God is present.

### *Prelude*

*The eternal God can only be experienced in the here and now, for everything in the universe is sustained by God's love in the present moment. When I worry about the past, or fret about the future, my consciousness of God, of creation, and of my deepest desires, is blocked. My challenge is to anchor both heart and mind **firmly** in the present: in each thought, word, and deed, as the story of my life evolves, in each moment, in God's presence.*

### *Illuminative Grace*

*Here I ask for what I desire: to be present and awake to every feeling, thought, word and deed – in the present moment.*
*I beg for the grace to wake up to God's presence in every person, experience, event – good or ill – that I encounter in my day.*

How lovely your dwelling, O Lord of hosts!
My Soul yearns and pines For the courts of the Lord.
My heart and flesh cry out For the living God.
As the sparrow finds a home and the swallow a nest to settle her young,
My home is by your altars Lord of hosts, my king and my God!
Blessed are those who dwell in your house!
They never cease to praise you.
(Ps. 84:2-5)

# MEMORY

*I believe every violation of love committed by me and against me **is in my memory, and I ask God to reveal them to me,** especially those that have manifested themselves today, **so I can be healed.***

### Prelude

*I hold in my heart, by the power of God's grace, the memory of every action – of every thought, word and deed – done to me and done by me, that has eroded my innocence. I affirm that these unloving thoughts, words and deeds have spiritual, physical, and emotional consequences that wound me, others, and creation and for which Christ had to suffer for my redemption. I believe all these unloving actions have both generational and evolutionary consequences. At the root of my own narcissism are some events that more than others, have more significantly distorted my heart and mind. These events cripple my desire and my ability to love selflessly and to freely forgive others.*

### Illuminative Grace

*Here I ask for what I desire: to become conscious of my lost innocence; the grace to see and the power to touch the Original Sins and wounds, especially the most vital ones, which shape in me and anti-story instead of a Sacred Story. I ask for the grace of an illumined conscience to know intimately how these wound and sins connect to **everything** I do that makes life burdensome; to know how and why these wounds so often complete me to violate God's life in myself, others and creation. I ask God for the grace to wake up so I can see, feel, and name these thoughts, words, and deeds, and bring them to the light of day, to be healed by the Divine Physician.*

Oh, that today you would hear his voice: "Harden not your hearts as at Meribah,
As in the day of Massah in the desert, Where your fathers tempted me; They test me thought they had seen my works. If today you hear his voice, Harden not your hearts.
(Ps 9:8-9)

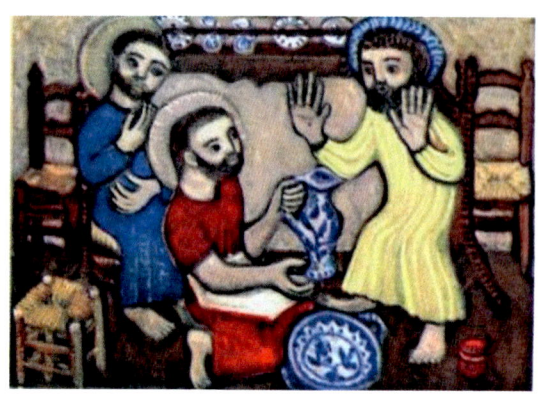

# MERCY

*I believe that **forgiveness** is the only **path to healing and illumination.** I beg for the **grace of forgiveness,** and the **grace to forgive,** especially for the general and particular failures of this day, and from my past.*

### *Prelude*

*The path to Christian holiness and an illumined consciousness runs through the darkest memories and deeds of your life, strangely enough. These memories and deeds corrupt your innocence and blind your vision to the sacredness of all life.*
*These memories and deeds can, by choice, act as a wall blocking the peace that leads to holiness and highest consciousness, or a as a gate opening to them.*
*The gate is unlocked by forgiveness and compassion; both received from God, and then extended to all those entwined with the lost innocence that broke your heart:*
*those who hurt you, those whom you hurt, and the gifts of creation that you abused or misused as a result. This miracle of peace and enlightenment is attainable through Christ, who core in love the wounds of every sin and dark deed since time immemorial. Christ has the power to transform darkness, sine and death into grace for the salvation of the world.*

### *Illuminative Grace*

*Here I ask for what I desire: For the grace to forgive any person who wounded my innocence, or who broke my heart. I pray to not only forgive them, but to have compassion and mercy on them. I ask for the grace of mercy and forgiveness for those whose hearts I have broken, and whose innocence I have wounded, and the gifts of creation that I have misused. I beg to know personally the One who absorbed in His heart and body every wound and every sin of this dark evolution across the millennia. I beg for the dual knowledge of sin and mercy as it affects my life story. I beg for patience, knowing that accepting and offering mercy and forgiveness leads me to holiness. This awakening to highest consciousness takes a lifetime.*

♥

Fill us at daybreak with your mercy, That all our days we may sing for joy.
Make us glad as many days as you humbled us, For as many years as we have seen trouble,
Show your deeds to your servants, your glory to their children.
(Ps 90:14-16)

**Theme Template: For three minutes write or draw pictures of what comes to mind in each catergory in your relationship with God.**

CREATION

PRESENCE

MEMORY

MERCY

Write a personal prayer asking God to open everyone in the class to serving His Kingdom of light and to be protected from serving the forces of darkness. Be specific in the prayer.

# LESSON TWO

**Objective:** Students will identify the right relationship/commandment and connect the First Commandment to the Right Relationship to give all my mind, heart, and strength to God alone and serve no other god by examining one's choices of use of time and money and reflecting on how current choices align with God being at the center of life with 100% student participation.

**Commandment 1/ Right Relationship**

*I am the Lord your God, you shall have no strange gods before me.*

*I believe God loved me into life and I commit to the relationship by giving all my mind, heart and strength to God alone and will serve no other god.*

As a child of God I am called **to keep Him at the center of my life by putting God first in all I do. If I forget that I am completely dependent on God, I will make idols of created goods. These idols can only enslave me.** I do not worship my accomplishments, my things or celebrities, remembering that God created me and gives me life each day.

**Action:** Each morning as I wake up I can say, "Good morning, (Father, Jesus, or Holy Spirit). This is _____, your friend."

| |
|---|
| • **Materials:** |
| ☐ Copies of the "The Golden Calf" reading |
| ☐ Poster of the Right Relationship for seventh grade |
| ☐ Computer |
| ☐ Projector |
| ☐ Internet access for PowerPoint |
| ☐ Candle |
| ☐ Directions for Word Clouds copied for students. If using computers the students will need internet access. |
| ☐ If doing homemade "word cloud" students will need at least one piece of paper and colored markers, poster board or butcher paper, glue. |
| ☐ Students will need markers or crayons or pen or pencil. |

Below is a picture of a word cloud. This can be made with the class by going to www.worditout.com. Detailed directions are in Addendum 2 Lesson 2. Search for other word cloud sites at http://www.edudemic.com/9-word-cloud-generators-that-arent-wordle/
Use this technological word cloud or create a homemade "word cloud" without a computer.

# LESSON TWO

**Post** the Right Relationship poster for all to see and for you to reference.

**Invitation to Prayer:**

The Golden Calf Exodus 32:1-26

*Light a candle and have the students sit in a circle with a copy of the prayer.*

*Start with the Sign of the Cross*

**Teacher:** *As we read the story of The Golden Calf from Exodus think of your relationship with people and things versus God's truth.*

Invite students to take turns reading a verse from Exodus 32:1-26

    a. The Ten Commandments are a gift from God to us. They help us know how we can create the right relationships to reconnect with God in our own Sacred Story. The first Three Commandments reveal God as our primary relationship because God is the origin and giver of all life. The command to love the Lord with all our mind, heart and strength is the only way we can have life because we are made in God's image and likeness. God made us to be in communion with God and it is the only path to life, happiness and peace.

    b. The last Seven Commandments affirm that being made in God's image and likeness, we are to love everyone God made as we would love and reverence our very self. By loving our neighbor as ourselves, we participate in God's loving plan for all of creation. Not to love our neighbor as ourselves is to break relationship with God because I break relationship with those made in God's image and likeness.

**Introduction: Whole Class Discussion or in small groups:**

Why did the Israelites create the "Golden Calf"?

What are our "Golden Calves" today? Teachers can opt for one of the following activities.

**Show PowerPoint about St. Ignatius of Loyola and his challenges with serving the one true God prior to his conversion at age 30.**

**Independent Practice:**

Option A. Using the list, students are to take time to reflect on how they use their time "My Golden Calves" Part One.

Then give time for students to complete "My Golden Calves" Part Two.

Discuss the results as a whole class or in small groups. Ask: Was there a difference between the two lists? If so, why is there a difference? How can we change what we do and have God at the center of our lives? What was the balance of their time and money? Note that none of these activities or way of spending money are wrong. The question is, are these replacing their time and focus on God?

What causes us to be distracted from God in our lives today? What are the things we do and spend our money on that are not focused on God? List ideas with students.

***There are two storylines to this relational paradigm: I can choose to serve the Lord of Life and Light and help build His Kingdom by only cooperating with the forces of light or***

***I can choose to serve the lord of darkness and death build his kingdom by cooperating with the forces of darkness—***

***No one can serve two masters.***


Option B. Do two word clouds: One that captures in single words lifestyles that serve the Lord of Light and another that captures in single words lifestyles that serve the lord of darkness.

Each child goes to word cloud website. An easy word cloud site is Worditout.com

*Or alternatively if you are not using computers:*

Each child writes of God on strip of paper and this is combined into a collage of God names by the students and teachers on the poster board/butcher paper or creates a http://www.tagxedo.com/app.htm

Invite students to share some of the word clouds.

**Closure:**

During our daily meditations we will be reflecting and then writing notes in Learning Logs. Our reflection will be:

*"Father, let me always be grateful for your gift of life and let me love all persons made in your image and likeness.*

*Let me always know what leads to life and what leads to death.*

*I know you will always be with me."*


**Read Deuteronomy 30:**

**I set before you this day, life and death, blessing and curse, therefore choose life that you and your descendants may live..."**

Your reflection is a time to reflect on how each of us can choose paths in "life" that lead to life and we can also choose paths that lead to "death"

# THE GOLDEN CALF

Exodus 32

When the people saw that Moses was delayed in coming down from the mountain, they gathered around Aaron and said to him, "Come, make us a god who will go before us; as for that man Moses who brought us out of the land of Egypt, we do not know what has happened to him."

Aaron replied, "Take off the golden earrings that your wives, your sons, and your daughters are wearing, and bring them to me." So all the people took off their earrings and brought them to Aaron. He received their offering, and fashioning it with a tool, made a molten calf. Then they cried out, "These are your gods, Israel, who brought you* up from the land of Egypt."

On seeing this, Aaron built an altar in front of the calf and proclaimed, "Tomorrow is a feast of the LORD." Early the next day the people sacrificed burnt offerings and brought communion sacrifices. Then they sat down to eat and drink, and rose up to revel.

Then the LORD said to Moses: Go down at once because your people, whom you brought out of the land of Egypt, have acted corruptly. They have quickly turned aside from the way I commanded them, making for themselves a molten calf and bowing down to it, sacrificing to it and crying out, "These are your gods, Israel, who brought you up from the land of Egypt!"

I have seen this people, how stiff-necked they are, continued the LORD to Moses. Let me alone, then, that my anger may burn against them to consume them. Then I will make of you a great nation.

But Moses implored the LORD, his God, saying, "Why, O LORD, should your anger burn against your people, whom you brought out of the land of Egypt with great power and with a strong hand?

Why should the Egyptians say, 'With evil intent he brought them out, that he might kill them in the mountains and wipe them off the face of the earth'? Turn from your burning wrath; change your mind about punishing your people.

Remember your servants Abraham, Isaac, and Israel, and how you swore to them by your own self, saying, 'I will make your descendants as numerous as the stars in the sky; and all this land that I promised, I will give your descendants as their perpetual heritage.'"

So the LORD changed his mind about the punishment he had threatened to inflict on his people.

Moses then turned and came down the mountain with the two tablets of the covenant in his hands, tablets that were written on both sides, front and back. The tablets were made by God; the writing was the writing of God, engraved on the tablets.

Now, when Joshua heard the noise of the people shouting, he said to Moses, "That sounds like a battle in the camp."

But Moses answered, "It is not the noise of victory, it is not the noise of defeat; the sound I hear is singing."

As he drew near the camp, he saw the calf and the dancing. Then Moses' anger burned, and he threw the tablets down and broke them on the base of the mountain. Taking the calf they had made, he burned it in the fire and then ground it down to powder, which he scattered on the water* and made the Israelites drink.

Moses asked Aaron, "What did this people do to you that you should lead them into a grave sin?" Aaron replied, "Do not let my lord be angry. You know how the people are prone to evil. They said to me, 'Make us a god to go before us; as for this man Moses who brought us out of the land of Egypt, we do not know what has happened to him.'

So I told them, 'Whoever is wearing gold, take it off.' They gave it to me, and I threw it into the fire, and this calf came out." Moses saw that the people were running wild because Aaron had lost control—to the secret delight of their foes.

Moses stood at the gate of the camp and shouted, "Whoever is for the LORD, come to me!" All the Levites then rallied to him.

**Directions for Word Cloud**

1. Go to www.Worditout.com
2. Click "CREATE" at the top of the page
3. Scroll down to "Enter Text"
4. Enter the words you wish to use such as: God Father Trinity. Note: The words are entered with spaces only
5. When finished entering the words click the green button on the upper right corner of the "Enter Text" section.
6. The word cloud appears. Scroll down and the word cloud size, color, text and other attributes can be changed.
7. Right click to print.
8. The word cloud can be saved in a cloud using an email address.

# "My Golden Calves" Part One

Below are some ways people spend their time. Add other activities that you do that may not be on the list. Write the approximate number of hours per week you engage in any of these activities.

| Activity | Hours per Week |
|---|---|

- A. School   _____
- B. Sports   _____
- C. Video games   _____
- D. Reading   _____
- E. Praying   _____
- F. Going to Mass   _____
- G. Service project   _____
- H. _____   _____
- I. _____   _____
- J. _____   _____

Below are some ways people spend their money. Add other items you usually buy that may not be on the list. Give a number to how you actually spend your money: 1 = at least once a week; 2 = once or more a month; 3 = once or more every few months; 4 = never.

| Expenditures | How you spend your money |
|---|---|

- A. Donations to Poor   _____
- B. Contributions to Church   _____
- C. Video games   _____
- D. Movies   _____
- E. Make Up   _____
- F. Clothes   _____
- G. Sports equipment   _____
- H. _____   _____
- I. _____   _____

# "My Golden Calves" Part Two

Below are some ways people spend their time. Add other activities that you do that may not be on the list. Write the approximate number of hours per week you should engage in any of these activities if God is at the center of your life.

**Activity**                    **Hours per Week**

- K.  School                    _____
- L.  Sports                    _____
- M.  Video games               _____
- N.  Reading                   _____
- O.  Praying                   _____
- P.  Going to Mass             _____
- Q.  Service project           _____
- R.  _____               _____
- S.  _____               _____
- T.  _____               _____

Below are some ways people spend their money. Add other items you usually buy that may not be on the list. Give a number to how you should spend your money if you are keeping God at the center of your decisions. 1 = at least once a week; 2 = once or more a month; 3 = once or more every few months; 4 = never.

**Expenditures**                **How you spend your money**

- J.  Donations to Poor         _____
- K.  Contributions to Church   _____
- L.  Video games               _____
- M.  Movies                    _____
- N.  Make Up                   _____
- O.  Clothes                   _____
- P.  Sports equipment          _____
- Q.  _____               _____
- R.  _____               _____

# RIGHT RELATIONSHIP

"I believe God loved me into life and I commit to the relationship by giving all my mind, heart and strength to God alone and will serve no other god."

# LESSON THREE

**Objective:** The student will be able to begin to discern God's voice in his/her life to reset his/her relationship with God, our source of life, who is love by fully participating in the meditation and reflection process with 100% participation.

> - **Materials:**
> - ☐ MP3 player
> - ☐ Computer
> - ☐ Internet access for meditation
> - ☐ Speakers
> - ☐ Copies of the learning logs for all students
> - ☐ Sacred Story Cross: If your class has the Sacred Story Cross please have students put the cubes in correct position: C, P, M & M for "Creation, Presence, Memory & Mercy" and "I" for the First Commandment.

# LESSON THREE

**Invitation to Prayer:**

Pray the **"Our Father"**

**Introduction:** Over the next few months we will practice meditation prayer to listen to God in our hearts and to deep and our conversation. As we meditate the center of our thoughts will be:

**I believe God loved me into life and I commit to the relationship by giving all my mind, heart and strength to God alone and will serve no other god.**

Our meditation themes are:

**CREATION, PRESENCE, MEMORY, MERCY and ETERNITY.**

Meditation is a prayer when people sit quietly and read or listen to God. It is a time for conversation with God in our hearts and in our minds. Over the next few months we will practice meditation prayer to listen to God in our hearts and to deep and our conversation. As we live we are allowing Christ to shape our *Sacred Story* through meditation.

God will use everything in your life to create your *Sacred Story*, even your most heinous mistakes. My discernment to keep or surrender is made according to whatever action advances me further along the path of my Sacred Story.

**Input:**

Ignatius names two spiritual states. One is *consolation* and the second is *desolation*.

**Consolation** – increase of faith, hope and love

**Desolation** - decrease of faith, hope and love.

Consolation is when we find a sense of peace that brings us closer to God.

God allows desolation, which is directly linked with your human growth and spiritual progress, to awaken your whole being-spirit, mind and body-to its spiritual, emotional and psychological wounds. Don't give up in times of spiritual desolation. This is the enemy's way of making us think that God does not care about you. During times of spiritual desolation it is more tempted to rely on oneself, but this is most definitely the time to turn to God and ask for help.

You are seeking the knowledge of your identify as a child of God, but informed by the truth of perfect relationship. Your authentic identity is a human nature, willed by God as unity of body and spirit.

Ultimately, you are seeking to know truth from falsehood in all of your thoughts, words and deeds.

**Guided Practice:**

"Let us discuss and decide on the environment we want to have while meditating." The teacher leads a class discussion on the following:

1. As we set aside this time for listening to God we need to be intentional about how we will pray. Together we will decide where we will meditate and what our classroom rules during this time will be. Then we will practice listening to a meditation.

   a. Where shall we meditate? Seats? Prayer rug?
   b. When shall we meditate? After morning recess? After lunch recess? Beginning of day?
   c. How shall we meditate? Let's establish our class rules for respecting each other's prayer time. Create a list of rules for meditation such as:
       1. Allow for silence in the room
       2. Sit comfortably and in my own space
       3. Participate
   d. Emphasize that we are together as a people but listening to God in our hearts. Note that for non-Catholics this can be a silent/peaceful time to reflect by oneself.

   e. **SACRED STORY CROSS**: If your class has the Sacred Story Cross please have students put the cubes in correct position. For seventh grade the "C" cube for "CREATION", "P" cube for PRESENCE, and "M" for MEMORY, "M" for MERCYs and the "I" for the First Commandment: "You Shall Serve The Lord Your God Alone and have no other gods before Him."

2. Preparing oneself to meditate:
    a. Think "I am aware that I can hear (i.e. the birds singing, students coughing, etc.) yes enter into silence with a few deep breaths.
3. At the end of the meditation time you will have an opportunity to record your thoughts for a minute or so in your learning logs.
4. You are now invited into the meditation space.
5. Practice quiet meditation with audio.\

Directions to teacher: go to Vimeo Meditation page.

(Learning logs are a record-keeping tool for students to monitor and reflect on their own learning. Learning logs differ from journals in that they focus on content covered in class, not students' personal and private feelings.) Students may reflect on how they feel, but it is always in relation to what is being studied in class. How to use the Learning Log:

- Listen to the meditation
- Have students write for one minute, no less and no more.
- Have students reread their learning log entries weekly and monthly.
- Teachers are advised to follow the policies of their district regarding learning logs.

6. Review what worked and how to improve the experience for all.

**Daily Meditations:**

**These should take about 6-8 minutes each day.**

**We suggest the meditations take place after morning or lunch recess. The time should be consistent each day and the meditations should be done every school day if possible.**

**To access the meditation there are two options:**

**1. Listen as a class: Teacher goes to Vimeo Meditation page.**
Have students prepare for meditation as discussed and planned with the class.
Students listen to the daily meditation.
Students complete learning log.

*OR*

**2. Listen individually with headphones**
Have students prepare for meditation as discussed and planned with the class.
Students listen to the daily meditation.
Students complete learning log.

*(Work should be done on following page)*

## SEVENTH GRADE

**Take one minute to draw or write a response to a Consolation and Desolation from the day's meditation.**

Let your heart write for you...it doesn't have to be perfect, but rather your meditations should reflect who you are and what you feel.

**I believe God loved me into life and I commit to the relationship by giving all my mind, heart and strength to God alone and will serve no other god.**

# CREATION, PRESENCE, MEMORY, MERCY

| | What increased your faith, hope and love? Be Specific! | What diminished your faith, hope and love? Be Specific! |
|---|---|---|
| MONDAY | | |
| TUESDAY | | |
| WEDNESDAY | | |
| THURSDAY | | |
| FRIDAY | | |

## Additional Ideas:

- ❖ Encourage students to get to know their weakness! List 3 embedded strengths they have (e.g. organization, discipline with study) and then 3 embedded weaknesses (bad temper, procrastination) and see how inspirations come through those sources in any given day.

- ❖ A parish priest suggested that we visualize one person we are thankful for and use this image during the Eucharistic Prayer at Mass. Ask students to draw a picture of themselves in a period of desolation (maybe under a dark cloud, or a dying tree a la Jonah) and name whether the emotion they are feeling is fear, anger or grief. Then, instead of acting on that feeling, what is their strategy in that moment for moving towards God rather than away from Him? Maybe an affirmation or a scripture or an arrow prayer.

- ❖ Follow up: Take time to revisit the purpose for the writing exercises; providing time for discussion about how spiritual desolation, if carefully attended to in thought, can provide the direction for behavior correction. Middle school students could offer personal examples of how we "learn from our mistakes".

# Certificate of Appreciation

This certificate is awarded to

**Sacred Story Institute**
Ignatian Spirituality for Third Millenium Evangelization

In recognition for participation in *Sacred Story Youth*

For more information visit www.sacredstory.net

Certificate of Appreciation

Teacher Signature _____ Date _____

*Fr. Bill Watson, President Sacred Story Institute*

# Teacher Theological Resource Guide

# Sacred Story Youth Program

# Foreword Inspirations

## Children in Scripture

O LORD, our Lord, how awesome is your name through all the earth!
I will sing of your majesty above the heavens with the mouths of babes and infants.
You have established a bulwark against your foes, to silence enemy and avenger.

Ps 8: 2

"See that you do not despise one of these little ones, for I say to you that their angels in heaven always look upon the face of my heavenly Father." Mt 18: 10

Then children were brought to him that he might lay his hands on them and pray.
The disciples rebuked them, but Jesus said, "Let the children come to me, and do not prevent them; for the kingdom of heaven belongs to such as these."

Mt 19: 13-14

Jesus said to them, "Yes; and have you never read the text,
'Out of the mouths of infants and nurslings you have brought forth praise'?"

Mt 21: 16

Taking a child he placed it in their midst, and putting his arms around it he said to them,
"Whoever receives one child such as this in my name, receives me;
and whoever receives me, receives not me but the One who sent me."

Mk 9: 36-37

Modern Missions to the Society of Jesus
From
The Supreme Pontiff
And
Apostolic Goals
From
Recent General Congregations

"To be truly Christian, our service to the Church must be anchored in fidelity to Christ, who makes all things new; to be proper to the Society, it must be done in union with the Successor of Peter.

1. To contribute effectively to the implementation of the Second Vatican Council;
2. To confront with all our forces the problem of atheism and cooperate in the profound renewal of the Church needed in a secularized age;
3. To better adapt our traditional apostolates to the different spiritual necessities of today: the renewal of Christian life, the education of youth, the formation of the clergy, the study of philosophy and theology, research into humanistic and scientific cultures, and missionary evangelization;
4. To pay particular attention to ecumenism, interreligious dialogue, and the task of authentic inculturation
5. In a manner consonant with our priestly and religious Institute and within the Church's evangelizing action, to promote the justice "connected with peace, which is the aspiration of all peoples";
6. To foster the vigorous impulse toward missionary work and church union and to serve our prophetic mission to promote the new evangelization.

✠ The pontifical mandate entrusted to the Society of resisting atheism should permeate all the accepted forms of our apostolate, in such wise that we may both cultivate among believers true faith and an authentic awareness of God and also zealously direct our efforts to nonbelievers of every type.[2]

✠ Certain fields of modern life have acquired a special urgency, fields that must be considered among the other works laudably carried on by our Society: c. the education of youth, especially those in greater need.
(GC 31 #375)

✠ Especially indeed ought we be concerned with areas critical for human person as a whole, such as the sciences of man and the education of youth. (GC 31 #409)

✠ In our day we are witnessing everywhere the rapid emergence of new social forms and the society of the future. When new ideas are so widely sown, it is not hard to discern the birth of new patterns of thought and action in the modern world. The promoters of these new ideas, especially when they work out of centers of higher culture and research, are exercising a mounting influence upon the whole of the social culture through highly effective modern means of popularization. But since this influence inclines ever more toward an atheistic and agnostic ideology and makes itself felt particularly in education centers, the presence of Christians in those centers is of the highest moment if the Church is indeed to make an opportune contribution to the society of the future by forming and educating its mind to reverence for God and in the fullness of Christ. (GC 31 # 497)

---

[2] *Constitutions of the Society of Jesus and Their Complimentary Norms.* Edited by John W. Padberg, SJ. St. Louis: Institute of Jesuit Sources, 277. Cited hereafter as *Constitutions.*

✠ For many centuries the Society of Jesus, in accordance with its Institute, has diligently exercised its teaching function almost uninterruptedly throughout the world. Now, impelled and inspired by the Second Vatican Council, the Society, through its 31st General Congregation, wishes to confirm the high regard it has for the apostolate of education and earnestly to exhort its members that they maintain unflaggingly their esteem for this significant apostolate. (GC 31 #498).

✠

*Whoever desires to serve as a soldier of God beneath the banner of the cross in our Society, which we desire to be designated by the name of Jesus, and to serve the Lord alone and the Church, his spouse, under the Roman pontiff, the vicar of Christ on earth, should, after a solemn vow of perpetual chastity, poverty, and obedience, keep what follows in mind. He is a member of a Society founded chiefly for this purpose: to strive especially for the defense and propagation of the faith and for the progress of souls in Christian life and doctrine, by means of public preaching, lectures, and any other ministration whatsoever of the word of God, and further by means of the Spiritual Exercises, the education of children and unlettered persons in Christianity, and the spiritual consolation of Christ's faithful through the hearing of confession and the administering the other sacraments.[3]*

---

[3] From the Jesuit: Formulas of the Institute, Constitutions 3-4.

# Inspirations from Recent Popes and Councils on Evangelization

## St John XXIII

✠

The major interest of the Ecumenical Council is this:
that the sacred heritage of Christian truth be safeguarded
and expounded with greater efficacy.

That doctrine embraces the whole man, body and soul.
It bids us live as pilgrims here on earth,
as we journey onwards towards our heavenly homeland.[4]

---

[4] Pope John XXIII: Opening Address to the Second Vatican Council

## *Lumen Gentium*-Second Vatican Council

✠

Christ is the Light of nations. Because this is so, this Sacred Synod gathered together in the Holy Spirit eagerly desires, by proclaiming the Gospel to every creature, to bring the light of Christ to all men, a light brightly visible on the countenance of the Church...

The present-day conditions of the world add greater urgency to this work of the Church so that all men, joined more closely today by various social, technical and cultural ties, might also attain fuller unity in Christ.[5]

---

[5] Lumen Gentium: Chapter 1, #1. Dogmatic Constitution on the Church

# Blessed Paul VI

✠

The obvious importance of the content of evangelization must not overshadow the importance of the ways and means.

This question of "how to evangelize" is permanently relevant, because the methods of evangelizing vary according to the different circumstances of time, place and culture, and because they thereby present a certain challenge to our capacity for discovery and adaptation.[6]

---
[6] Pope Paul VI: Evangelii Nuntiandi, 1975, #40.

## St. John Paul II

✠

Let us go forward in hope!
A new millennium is opening before the Church like a vast ocean upon which we shall venture, relying on the help of Christ.
The Son of God, who became incarnate two thousand years ago out of love for humanity, is at work even today:
we need discerning eyes to see this and, above all,
a generous heart to become the instruments of his work.[7]

---
[7] Apostolic letter: *Novo Millennio Ineunte* of his holiness Pope John Paul II (2000) #58.

# Benedict XVI

✠

"We no longer know how to communicate effectively the truths of our faith. They are still true, but not understood. We must come up with entirely new ways to preach to the people of our own day."[8]

---

[8] Pope Benedict quoted in the 2010 last full book length interview he did with the German reporter, Peter Sewall: "The Light of the World"

Pope Francis

✠

I ask you, instead, to be revolutionaries, to swim against the tide; yes, I am asking you to rebel against this culture that sees everything as temporary and that ultimately believes that you are incapable of responsibility, that you are incapable of true love. Do not be afraid to go and to bring Christ into every area of life, to the fringes of society, even to those who seem farthest away, most indifferent. The Church needs you, your enthusiasm, your creativity and the joy that is so characteristic of you.[9]

---
[9] Pope Francis, Rio 2013, World Youth Day

# Introduction

Each religious order in the Church has its own saint's feast days and special readings for those feasts. The first reading chosen for the feast of St. Ignatius Loyola is from the thirtieth chapter of the Book of Deuteronomy, verses sixteen to twenty. In the New American Bible, the section is titled: *The Choice before Israel*. In truth, it is the choice set before every person, no matter their age or beliefs. It says in part:

> *I have set before you life and death, the blessing and the curse. Choose life, then, that you and your descendants may live, by loving the LORD, your God, obeying his voice, and holding fast to him. For that will mean life for you, a long life for you to live on the land which the LORD swore to your ancestors, to Abraham, Isaac, and Jacob, to give to them.*

The reading is chosen to reflect the gift of spiritual discernment God left to the Church in St. Ignatius Loyola. For thirty years, he lived a life with himself, not God, at the center. He awakened from his self-centered fantasies by the grace of God who attuned St. Ignatius to his interior affective states of happiness and sadness. He discovered by how he felt, what was from God and what was from the one he titled "the enemy of human nature." What he discovered is the choice God set before Israel. There are only two choices in life that each of us has. One set of choices and one identity leads to God and the other leads away: life or death, blessing or curse.

The purpose of the *Sacred Story Youth* program is to teach the interior listening skills God taught to St. Ignatius to our youngest believers. We already give them the content of what we believe in so many wonderful ways. We need to be sure that we are teaching them they are spiritual beings who have spiritual radar for right and wrong that can be accessed by simply paying attention to the state of our hearts.

Our evangelization must touch the mind and the heart and introduce people to the person of Christ. Evangelization for our youth that relies principally the content of the faith without fostering a personal relationship with Christ that is heart-felt will not create intentional disciples. Sheri Weddell in her book, *Forming Intentional Disciples*, points out 70% of all adults who go through RCIA leave after the first year. The statistics for youth who fall away from faith practice after Confirmation programs is nearly has high. And writers like Christian Smith, a Roman Catholic, and David Kinnaman, an Evangelical, reveal how we are losing our youngest believers by the pressures of the secular culture and ineffective methods of communicating the person of Jesus Christ in our faith formation.[10]

This interior freedom for service is the hallmark of Ignatian Spirituality and the goal of *Sacred Story Youth*. Ignatius' practice of the daily *Examen*, and the interior freedom it brought him, changed the history of the Church and the world. Imagine what a handful of people in every religious community, parish, high school and university around the earth could accomplish by living it daily.

IMAGINE the transformation of Church and society we can achieve in Christ by teaching our youth how to day connect with Christ and discern His voice in their hearts! When we help our youth discover the voice of God in their hearts and daily stay connected to him in a heart-felt relationship, they can serve Him in freedom and His Kingdom—living life as a *Sacred Story*.

Be Not Afraid!

---

[10] See: *Lost in Transition: The Dark Side of Emerging Adulthood* by Christian Smith and, *You Lost Me: Why Young Christians are Leaving Church and Rethinking Faith*, by David Kinnaman.

# Chapter One

## A SIMPLE CATECHESIS ON CREATION AND THE FALL

*Our Amazing "Created" Universe*

The *Sacred Story* of Creation began thirteen point seven billion years ago, give or take a hundred million years. We have only mapped galaxies out to one hundred million light years; the remaining thirteen point six billion light years to the burst at creation's origins is beyond our *vision*. But all that is "seen and unseen" in the universe came to be…from *nothing*. Time and space was *created!* It was not, and then it was. When you pray, think of Creation as the beginning of the SACRED STORY. Let the awesomeness of this truth create wonder in your heart. Ponder its meaning and always, give thanks.

The *Sacred Story* of Creation had another beginning four point five billion years ago. Earth came into existence: the densest of eight planets of a small solar system in the Orion Arm on the outer reaches of the Milky Way Galaxy. A rare combination of events enables this beautiful orb to produce complex intelligent life. We are the perfect distance from the center and edge of our galaxy. Our position enables us to escape the center's dangerous radiation and crowding that would disrupt the delicate orbital axis around our star. If we were any further out however, we would be deficient in the heavy metals produced by the supernovas of the galactic center.

As a small planet, we have a dense, unusually large moon that stabilizes the 23° tilt of earth's rotation axis, holding it steady in this position for millions of years. Without the moon as anchor, Jupiter and Saturn would cause a wild orbit, with massive climate changes and an environment hostile to complex life. Without a planet the size of Jupiter, we would be ten thousand times more exposed to the violent strikes of asteroids and meteors that would sterilize the planet, making it unable to sustain life. There has not been one such strike for two point five billion years.

Earth has had two total ice events; one, two point five billion years ago and another, five hundred and fifty million years ago. The first ice event created conditions for single cell life to expand. The second event, at the time of the Cambrian explosion, conspired to transform single cell life into complex multi-cellular life. The earth possesses rare plate tectonics that produce a remarkably stable temperature regulation mechanism, enabling the evolution of complex life.[11]

In spite of all we know about the human person, science cannot really answer the most basic questions of how life works. How does the mind work? What is DNA? Why/how do cells function the way they do? Why is loving, human physical contact necessary for a baby's physical and mental development? How and why does the immaterial spirit (or mind) powerfully impact the material biochemical processes in our cells and vice versa? Just what is *human nature*, the name our tradition gives to the divinely created unity of body/spirit? How does *human nature* work?

We have a better understanding of life's mechanics, but comprehending why life works the way it does is far beyond our capacities. The more we observe of the body and the mind's workings, the more unbelievable life appears.[12] We can't even explain how a minute sequoia seed develops into the largest living thing on earth. When you pray with Creation in *Sacred Story*, remember your human life is a miracle that even the most brilliant scientific minds can't explain. Let the awesomeness of this truth create wonder in your heart. Ponder its meaning. Give thanks.

---

[11] Inspired by: *Rare Earth: Why Complex Life is Uncommon in the Universe,* by Peter Ward and Donald Brownlee. Ward and Brownlee have both taught at the University of Washington.

[12] Inspired by: *The Cell's Design* by Fazale Rana; *Everything You Need to Feel Go(o)d,* by Candace B. Pert, Ph.D.; *The First Gene,* by David L. Abel, Editor; *The Spiritual Brain* by Mario Beauregard; *Touching, The Human Significance of the Skin,* by Ashley Montagu; and personal conversations with Mr. Jim Harding of CODONiS.com.

Our Faith affirms that God created the cosmos *ex-nihilo* — from nothing. We can affirm this Divine act of creation was an act of Love. God is Love (1 Jn 4:8). God created human persons, women and men, to share in this love and in love's creative energy. For marital love offers husbands and wives a share in God's loving, creative genius. A child is born who will live for eternity. Have you ever contemplated this profound mystery: the creative power God gives to women and men? An eternal being is born in time. When you pray with Creation in *Sacred Story*, remember your human life is an *ex-nihilo* act of Love from God through your parents. You did not have to *be*, but Love desired that you be born. Creation is an act of Love. You are born by God's act of Love shared with your parents. Let the awesomeness of this truth create wonder in your heart. Ponder its meaning. Give thanks.

If a person had the occasion to ask God one question, it might be; "WHY? Why did you create all of this?" Perhaps God's response would be; "Because I thought it would delight you." In the end, we can reach no other conclusion for creation. The remarkable, awesome and beautiful universe we are privileged to delight in was God's *deliberate choice* — a gratuitous gift by Love to share love. It is *all* a gift from Love itself. Creation is love made visible. *Human beings* are the height of God's creation; persons who can give and receive God's love. In our loving, we become co-creators with God. Jesus Christ is Love itself poured out in complete humility to be Emmanuel, "*God with us*." Love, The Infinite One, The Almighty, The Creator of all has become one of us! Love itself, sharing Love with us creatures made in Love's Divine image. We are empowered by Love to create in love, other beings who will also be able to love. Love is the source of all creative energy. Let the awesomeness of this truth create wonder in your heart. Ponder its meaning. Give thanks.


*God is a Sacred Diversity of Persons Made One by a Communion of Love*[13]

The current doctrine of the Blessed Trinity, our belief in three persons but one God, reached is final form in the late 4th century. Some of the most sophisticated theological writings in the history of the Church are devoted to discussions about the nature of the One God in Three Persons and the Three Persons in One God.

---

[13] For a complete on-line definition of the Doctrines on the Trinity see: http://www.catholic.org/encyclopedia/view.php?id=11699

If you want to look up the history of the development of this foundational creed of the Christian faith, follow the link below to the Catholic Encyclopedia on-line for a full history of the doctrine.[14]

When we look the Trinity with fresh eyes we can help a new generation unlock the mysteries of the universe! For God is Relationship and God creates a relational universe. For God's most essential Nature is Relationship: three distinct Persons made One by a Communion in Love. We might even say that Being—Existence—is LOVE. The Communion of Persons in Love has no beginning or end for Love is eternal!

> *Beloved, let us love one another, because love is of God; everyone who loves is begotten by God and knows God. Whoever is without love does not know God,* **for God is love.** (1 John 4 7-8)

Love is only possible in the presence of distinct persons who can give and receive love. The unique, distinct Persons of the Trinity freely and without boundaries, give and receive Love. It is this utter and complete Communion that makes them ONE. And the Communion is LOVE! The ability to retain individuality yet be in complete communion with the "other" can only happen in the presence of complete love.

*Creation is Relational and An Act of Love*

Our faith affirms that God created the cosmos *ex-nihilo* — from nothing.[15] We hold as truth that everything in the spiritual and material cosmos came from nothing but issued forth from God through the Son—The WORD who was with God in the Beginning. The Nicene Creed states:

*I believe in one God, the Father, the Almighty, maker of heaven and earth, and of all that is, seen and unseen.*
*We believe in one Lord, Jesus Christ, the only Son of God, eternally begotten of the Father, God from God,*
*Light from Light, true God from true God,*
*begotten, not made, one in Being with the Father.*

---

[14] Here is the summary of the doctrine of the Trinity from our Church's Catechism. "The mystery of the Most Holy Trinity is the central mystery of the Christian faith and of Christian life. God alone can make it known to us by revealing himself as Father, Son and Holy Spirit. The Incarnation of God's Son reveals that God is the eternal Father and that the Son is consubstantial with the Father, which means that, in the Father and with the Father the Son is one and the same God. The mission of the Holy Spirit, sent by the Father in the name of the Son (Jn 14:26) and by the Son "from the Father" (Jn 15:26), reveals that, with them, the Spirit is one and the same God. "With the Father and the Son he is worshipped and glorified" (Nicene Creed). "The Holy Spirit proceeds from the Father as the first principle and, by the eternal gift of this to the Son, from the communion of both the Father and the Son". By the grace of Baptism "in the name of the Father and of the Son and of the Holy Spirit", we are called to share in the life of the Blessed Trinity, here on earth in the obscurity of faith, and after death in eternal light. "Now this is the Catholic faith: We worship one God in the Trinity and the Trinity in unity, without either confusing the persons or dividing the substance; for the person of the Father is one, the Son's is another, the Holy Spirit's another; but the Godhead of the Father, Son and Holy Spirit is one, their glory equal, their majesty coeternal" Inseparable in what they are, the divine persons are also inseparable in what they do. But within the single divine operation each shows forth what is proper to him in the Trinity, especially in the divine missions of the Son's Incarnation and the gift of the Holy Spirit." CCC: 261-267.

[15] A good video on the creation of the universe has been produced by Fr. Robert Spitzer's Magis Center. You can find the *From Nothing to Cosmos –God and Science* here: http://vimeo.com/magiscenter/review/89120411/080cbf77e7

*Through him all things were made.*

The one *from whom all things were made* is the principal in which all things in creation—spiritual and material—cohere. This Person, One in Being with the Father, is the Word of Life. We read in John 1: 1-3:

*In the beginning was the Word,*
*and the Word was with God,*
*and the Word was God.*
*He was in the beginning with God.*
*All things came to be through him,*
*and without him nothing came to be.*
*What came to be through him was life,*
*and this life was the light of the human race;*
*the light shines in the darkness,*
*and the darkness has not overcome it.*

Our creedal faith also affirms that God not only created the cosmos, but God created *all that is*, "seen and unseen." God created a visible cosmos yet also a whole hierarchy of spiritual beings who are "unseen" but real. This "unseen" spiritual world we accept as truth.[16]

We can affirm this Divine act of creation through the Word was an act of Love. For God is Love (1 Jn 4:8). God created unseen spiritual beings and human persons, women and men, to participate and share in love and in love's creative energy. For human persons are made in God's image and likeness. Read Genesis 1: 26-28:

*Then God said: Let us make human beings in our image, after our likeness. Let them have dominion over the fish of the sea, the birds of the air, the tame animals, all the wild animals, and all the creatures that crawl on the earth. God created mankind in his image; in the image of God he created them; male and female he created them. God blessed them and God said to them: Be fertile and multiply; fill the earth and subdue it. Have dominion over the fish of the sea, the birds of the air, and all the living things that crawl on the earth.*

*A Sacred Diversity of Beings Made One by Communion with God*

God not only created human persons with a human nature but with a unity of body and spirit. God also created persons of unique gender specifically for the purpose of sharing love in communion and participating

---

[16] For a discussion of this "unseen" spiritual world, access the Catechism of the Catholic Church online here: http://www.vatican.va/archive/ccc_css/archive/catechism/p1s2c1p5.htm

in God's creative powers.[17] Marital love offers husbands and wives a share in God's loving, creative genius.[18] God also made us to be in harmonious communion with each other, each made in God's image. This was the original plan of God.[19] This was Jesus' command/desire at the last supper that we recover our original destiny:

> *"I pray not only for them, but also for those who will believe in me through their word, so that they may all be one, as you, Father, are in me and I in you, that they also may be in us, that the world may believe that you sent me. (Jn 17: 21).*

If a person had the occasion to ask God one question, it might be; "WHY? Why did you create all of this?" Perhaps God's response would be; "Because I thought it would delight you." In the end, we can reach no other conclusion for creation than God's gratuitous desire to share love.

The remarkable, awesome and beautiful universe we are privileged to delight in was God's *deliberate choice*—a gratuitous gift by Love to share love and life with us beings made in God's image and likeness. It is *all* a gift from Love itself. Creation is love made visible. And human persons are beings fashioned in God's own likeness—to be unique persons called to a full communion of love with God and with each other. This is what paradise as depicted in Genesis was *in essence*.

---

[17] *Equality and difference willed by God* Man and woman have been created, which is to say, willed by God: on the one hand, in perfect equality as human persons; on the other, in their respective beings as man and woman. "Being man" or "being woman" is a reality which is good and willed by God: man and woman possess an inalienable dignity which comes to them immediately from God their Creator. Man and woman are both with one and the same dignity "in the image of God". In their "being-man" and "being-woman", they reflect the Creator's wisdom and goodness.
In no way is God in man's image. He is neither man nor woman. God is pure spirit in which there is no place for the difference between the sexes. But the respective "perfections" of man and woman reflect something of the infinite perfection of God: those of a mother and those of a father and husband.
*"Each for the other" - "A unity in two"* God created man and woman together and willed each for the other. The Word of God gives us to understand this through various features of the sacred text. "It is not good that the man should be alone. I will make him a helper fit for him." None of the animals can be man's partner. The woman God "fashions" from the man's rib and brings to him elicits on the man's part a cry of wonder, an exclamation of love and communion: "This at last is bone of my bones and flesh of my flesh." Man discovers woman as another "I", sharing the same humanity.
Man and woman were made "for each other" - not that God left them half-made and incomplete: he created them to be a communion of persons, in which each can be "helpmate" to the other, for they are equal as persons ("bone of my bones. . .") and complementary as masculine and feminine. In marriage God unites them in such a way that, by forming "one flesh", they can transmit human life: "Be fruitful and multiply, and fill the earth." By transmitting human life to their descendants, man and woman as spouses and parents co-operate in a unique way in the Creator's work.
In God's plan man and woman have the vocation of "subduing" the earth as stewards of God. This sovereignty is not to be an arbitrary and destructive domination. God calls man and woman, made in the image of the Creator "who loves everything that exists", to share in his providence toward other creatures; hence their responsibility for the world God has entrusted to them. (Catechism of the Catholic Church #369-373. [From here forward identified by "CCC."]

[18] Have you ever contemplated this profound mystery: the creative power God gives to women and men? An eternal being is born in time-a child is born who will live for eternity. When we contemplate Creation, remember that your human life is an ex-nihilo act of Love from God through your parents. You did not have to *be*, but Love desired that you be born. Creation is an act of Love. You are born by God's act of Love shared with your parents. Let the awesomeness of this truth create wonder in your heart. Ponder its meaning. Give thanks.

[19] Because of its common origin *the human race forms a unity*, for "from one ancestor [God] made all nations to inhabit the whole earth." (*Acts* 17:26; cf. *Tob* 8:6.) CCC #360.

*The Original Sin Destroys Immortality and God' Relational World*

God not only gave us life when he made us but God also gifted us with immortality. God gave human persons an eternal soul. Human nature, body and soul conjoined, is a gift of God. Many of us forget to reflect that the paradise depicted in Genesis was of beings made in God's image and likeness, but also of beings that were immortal. Our human nature which is itself a relationship comprised of body and spirit was "made" that way by God so we can "commune" with God.[20]

We are, therefore, enfleshed spirits who have been gifted with a spiritual nature to enjoy life and love in relationship with God who is Love and Life. The source and condition of our immortality was that we remain in *full spiritual communion* with God.

Both the unseen spiritual world and the visible creation of persons made in God's image and likeness formed the sacred diversity intended by God from the beginning. This sacred diversity was made possible by beings who freely remained devoted and in communion with the Creator God. Diverse beings—inimitable personalities—could rejoice in their diverseness and yet, like the Trinity, be in full communion with each other. This communion in diversity was possible because of each individual's devotion and full communion with the God who is love. Diversity is sacred when beings made in God's image and likeness are in communion with God.

*The Rise of an Unholy Diversity Opposed to God*

---

[20] II. "BODY AND SOUL BUT TRULY ONE"
The human person, created in the image of God, is a being at once corporeal and spiritual. The biblical account expresses this reality in symbolic language when it affirms that "then the LORD God formed man of dust from the ground, and breathed into his nostrils the breath of life; and man became a living being."[Gen 2:7] Man, whole and entire, is therefore willed by God.
In Sacred Scripture the term "soul" often refers to human life or the entire human person. But "soul" also refers to the innermost aspect of man, that which is of greatest value in him, that by which he is most especially in God's image: "soul" signifies the spiritual principle in man.

The human body shares in the dignity of "the image of God": it is a human body precisely because it is animated by a spiritual soul, and it is the whole human person that is intended to become, in the body of Christ, a temple of the Spirit: Man, though made of body and soul, is a unity. Through his very bodily condition he sums up in himself the elements of the material world. Through him they are thus brought to their highest perfection and can raise their voice in praise freely given to the Creator. For this reason man may not despise his bodily life. Rather he is obliged to regard his body as good and to hold it in honour since God has created it and will raise it up on the last day. The unity of soul and body is so profound that one has to consider the soul to be the "form" of the body: i.e., it is because of its spiritual soul that the body made of matter becomes a living, human body; spirit and matter, in man, are not two natures united, but rather their union forms a single nature.

The Church teaches that every spiritual soul is created immediately by God - it is not "produced" by the parents - and also that it is immortal: it does not perish when it separates from the body at death, and it will be reunited with the body at the final Resurrection.
Sometimes the soul is distinguished from the spirit: St. Paul for instance prays that God may sanctify his people "wholly", with "spirit and soul and body" kept sound and blameless at the Lord's coming. The Church teaches that this distinction does not introduce a duality into the soul. "Spirit" signifies that from creation man is ordered to a supernatural end and that his soul can gratuitously be raised beyond all it deserves to communion with God.

The spiritual tradition of the Church also emphasizes the heart, in the biblical sense of the depths of one's being, where the person decides for or against God. CCC # 362-368.

Turning from full communion with God inaugurates the fall of creation's sacred diversity. It is the separation from Love which destroys relationships and unleashes upon the cosmos and the world a virus of anti-love—anti-Christ—that can destroy relationships at every level in God's creation.[21] As Christians, we hold as truth this rebellion to freely turn from God happened first in beings that were purely spiritual in nature.[22]

Only the choice to freely turn from God, who is Life, and Love of God can initiate a fall from grace that brings evil into the cosmos and the world. For evil to infect the material world a spiritual portal was needed. And that portal had to be persons whose human nature was physical and spiritual. The temptation to turn from full communion with God was an appeal to those with a human nature by the spiritual being our tradition calls Satan.[23] This spiritual being St. Ignatius calls the enemy of human nature.

No other force in the known cosmos can unify humanity in the order of Creation except the One who created it. Once the choice was made to turn from full communion with God, the holy communion of sacred diversity will be gradually eroded. It was the enemy of human nature's plan to create an unholy diversity of individuals who have become their own gods, take the law upon themselves and guide them in their pride to destroy human life and all creation.

God is Life and Satan is Death. God is Relationship and Satan is anti-relationship. God is Love and Satan is self-love. God creates and Satan destroys. God is truth and Satan is falsehood. God is One and Satan is a legion. God's diversity creates harmony, Satan's diversity creates chaos and destruction. An anti-God and anti-human nature power is unleashed by the primeval disobedience of Original Sin and will alter evolution's course. Guided by human nature's enemy, persons whose god is the self, following base instincts will threaten human life and all creation.

Seeing this reality up close after the devastation of WWI, the poet William Butler Yeats composed his poem The Second Coming:

> *Turning and turning in the widening gyre*
> *The falcon cannot hear the falconer;*
> *Things fall apart; the center cannot hold;*

---

[21] Anti-Love or Anti-Christ is the essence of anti-relationship. This anti-relationship or *self*-centeredness, as opposed to God-centeredness, spells eternal condemnation for spiritual beings and physical death to incarnate spirits.

[22] You can read what we believe as true about the fall of the angels and the fall of humankind in the *Catechism of the Catholic Church* online here: http://www.vatican.va/archive/ccc_css/archive/catechism/p1s2c1p7.htm

[23] "Behind the disobedient choice of our first parents lurks a seductive voice, opposed to God, which makes them fall into death out of envy.266 Scripture and the Church's Tradition see in this being a fallen angel, called "Satan" or the "devil".267 The Church teaches that Satan was at first a good angel, made by God: "The devil and the other demons were indeed created naturally good by God, but they became evil by their own doing." (Lateran Council IV (1215): DS 800). From Catechism of the Catholic Church #391.

> *Mere anarchy is loosed upon the world,*
> *The blood-dimmed tide is loosed, and everywhere*
> *The ceremony of innocence is drowned;*
> *The best lack all conviction, while the worst*
> *Are full of passionate intensity.*
>
> *Surely some revelation is at hand;*
> *Surely the Second Coming is at hand.*
> *The Second Coming! Hardly are those words out*
> *When a vast image out of Spiritus Mundi*[24]
> *Troubles my sight: somewhere in sands of the desert*
> *A shape with lion body and the head of a man,*
> *A gaze blank and pitiless as the sun,*
> *Is moving its slow thighs, while all about it*
> *Reel shadows of the indignant desert birds.*
> *The darkness drops again; but now I know*
> *That twenty centuries of stony sleep*
> *Were vexed to nightmare by a rocking cradle,*
> *And what rough beast, its hour come round at last,*
> *Slouches towards Bethlehem to be born?*

Yeats' imagery of the falcon circling further and further from the falconer is a metaphor of individuals getting further and further from the voice of God. In these outlands, far from paradise, the instincts of our lower appetites will rule the day and "the ceremony of innocence is drowned."[25] Our sensibilities are still shocked at the violation of innocence and youth.

We must remember that this rape of innocence—that begins with the loss of the innocence of our first parents and the breaking of their relationship with the Creator—is *the* distinguishing characteristic of Satan's seduction in the Original Sin. It was the archetypal, primeval abduction of the sacred innocence of the children of paradise from the heavenly Father. It was the attempted destruction of the world of joyful, innocent love gifted to human nature by God. The result of disobedience and the silencing of God from the human heart in the Original Sin's loss of innocence created the condition where "the falcon cannot hear the falconer." Conscience is silenced. The children of paradise have been banished: a tragedy shocking to the heart of God. Yes, in this new frightening world "things fall apart; the center cannot hold!"

---

[24] This would be "the Spirit of the World," an image of Satan as ruler of the world.
[25] The musical artists, Joni Mitchell, put Yeats' poem to music. You can listen to it here on YouTube: http://www.youtube.com/watch?v=f1j0j4r_gnw

The novelist Stephen King has his own take on a world unhinged with human hearts cut off from God and where the "self" is god. The novel is called *Needful Things.* In the story, everyone in this small New England town purchases items from a new shop called "Needful Things." Each item desired and purchased characterizes the individual's lusts and pulls them into themselves and away from others. They literally "sell their souls" to get the items they want the most. The proprietor is named Leland Gaunt (Satan, of course).

As the narrative unfolds, we see the town descending into utter chaos and destruction as people war with each other. The moral is when we all become our own gods and satisfy our most base instincts, individual and socially, things fracture. A type of diversity whereby each person becomes their own god, follow their "own way" is exactly what Satan planned from the first temptation.

Another novelist, Suzanne Collins, has depicted a dystopian world set in a not-to-distant future United States. Any grade school teacher today will know of Collins and the popularity with young children of her *Hunger Games* trilogy.[26] In Collins' future world, human life is cheap and the experience of it for the vast majority is predatory. Powerful elites, confined in protected wealthy enclaves keep the masses in line with Roman Circus styled games where young people kill each other on live television. Many commentators have suggested that such a dark vision of American is so popular with youth is that many of them intuit it as a reality in their own lives.

Early in my career at Georgetown University in the mid-1980's, I had a discussion with John Griffith, MD, the new VP for the Georgetown Hospital and Medical School. John, aRoman Catholic physician, said he was concerned about how medical ethics was developing. He said we are re-writing the rules of what constitutes "valuable human life" at both birth and old age. He said when you rewrite of the laws of what constitutes human life at both ends of the spectrum it will only be a matter of time before the line on what constitutes "valuable life" would move toward the center from both poles. What he meant is once life as an "absolute" value is done away with, it is only a matter of time before all human life is threatened. When we speak about "rights" in the context of both abortion and death—the rights to reproductive freedom and right to die—then we know we have crossed the line.

These "freedoms" and "rights" now enshrined in many of our laws are exactly the "freedoms" and "rights" envisioned by creation's destroyer at the start of it all. Satan deceived our first parents as he knew the "apparent good" he was suggesting would lead to utter chaos and destruction. As Jesus says of Satan in Scripture:

> "*You belong to your father, the devil, and you willingly carry out your father's desires. He was a murderer from the beginning and does not stand in truth, because there is no truth in him.*

---

[26] The three books in trilogy are: *The Hunger Games*; *Catching Fire* and *Mockingjay*. All books published by Scholastic. Collins has become the all-time best-selling Kindle author through Amazon.com.

> *When he tells a lie, he speaks in character, because he is a liar and the father of lies. He was a murderer from the beginning. (Jn 8:44)*

The "fall" resulted from the free choice to turn from full communion with God. all beings made by God had the choice to turn from God; this was their "birthright." This is especially true of those whose human nature was crafted in God's image and likeness. Love can only be freely accepted or rejected; love cannot be forced.

But for those with a human nature that is spiritual and physical, *full communion* with the Creator God who is Life and Love is the condition for immortality. Creation's diversity only maintains its sanctity when beings with a free will choose to remain in full communion with God. For only full communion with God provides the basis for distinct persons to both fully maintain their individuality while being fully in communion with others.

*The Three Stages of the Original Sin Set the Template for Every Sin*

In the true allegory of paradise depicted in the book of Genesis, God walks in the garden in the cool of the evening expressing in poetic images the complete union man and woman experienced with God. There were no barriers of any kind, only full communion with God and with each other and with creatures. They loved and obeyed God. Righteousness and truth governed all relationships in paradise. Adam and Eve walked side by side in loving harmony, for they knew and followed *only* the voice of God. This is the way God intended woman and man to relate to him, to each other and to all of creation.

We must understand the strategy utilized by the enemy of human nature to turn Adam and Eve from God as their life and love to self as life and love. Pay close attention to how he the Original Sin is staged. It has three stages and every sin in the history of the world will follow the same pattern.

## FIRST STAGE
*Turning from God's Voice and From the Truth of Their Hearts*
*They Violate Covenant Obedience*

Adam and Eve walked in harmony and union with God in paradise. But a tragic new reality begins when the serpent, the "other" opposed to God's mission, enters the story. Lucifer, the great angel who opposed God, is cast from heaven along with those spirits who joined with him. Hating God and God's plans, he is determined not only to destroy God's creation but also God's creatures, man and woman, made in God's image.

The deceiver must insert himself between God and Adam and Eve to tempt them to follow him. This is the precise strategy we affirm Satan used with the other spirits who stopped listening to God's voice and chose to side with the mission of anti-love opposed to God. This is the origin of the theological concept of the anti-Christ, the one(s) opposed to God's plan and mission for humankind and the universe.

But for temptation to gain a foothold in paradise, the serpent must first establish a relationship with Adam and Eve, and he does this by "speaking" to them in their hearts. Remember, human persons are gifted with a spiritual nature that is capable of communing with the God and the entire spiritual realm. Eve and Adam open themselves to temptation by "listening" in their hearts to the serpent. By their very listening to the Tempter's "voice," they place his voice and suggestions on equal footing with the voice and commands of God.[27]

We think of Adam and Eve as adults, but our understanding of adulthood has been corrupted by the history of so much sin in the world. Adam and Eve were innocent, like children are innocent. Evil always seeks to corrupt the innocent by clever and subtle invitations. The corruption begins by first getting the innocent to "listen" to new ideas that ever so subtly violate the order of God's creation, God's plan, and God's mission.[28]

Listening indicates their openness to a relationship with the Tempter and displaces God's voice as the only "voice of the heart." The Latin word for *obey* means to *listen deeply*. This is precisely what Adam and Eve have now failed to do. Inviting into their hearts and minds a new voice divides their hearts and minds. In essence, their inviting in of another voice is a failure to be obedient. The first level of sin is a violation of the vow of obedience, for Adam and Eve were to listen only to the voice of God.

Let's think of how this first level of temptation and sin affects children at the "age of reason." Consider good and loving parents whose obedient child is being tempted for the first time. The temptation comes from someone (an adult, another child, the Tempter) as a new and different voice with a new and different offer, perhaps inviting the child to consider a different way of behaving from what they have been taught by their "good" parents. There is always a first time when as young children in possession of reason and will, we first

---

[27] We are reminded of the cartoon image of a person with an angel on one shoulder and a devil on the other, each proposing a different choice. The truth in the image is that every person can "listen" to the voice of God speaking in heart and conscience or to the voice of the one St. Ignatius calls "the enemy of human nature."

*hear*, and then *listen to another voice*-one that is very different from the "truth" we know and possess in our hearts.[29]

## SECOND STAGE
### Cut-off from God's Truth They See and Desire Unholy Experiences
### They Violate Covenant Chastity

After disobeying God by "listening" to the voice of the Tempter, Adam and Eve look upon their Paradise with different eyes. Of course what they "see" and "desire" will be far different than when their hearts were fully united with God. In fact, they will see and desire things that are new to them.

The Tempter proposes they "see" the fruit of the Tree of Good and Evil as *good* for eating. The Tempter appeals to human pride, instructing them that they will be *like gods* if they eat this fruit. Pride turns us from trusting God. Pride is *self*-reliance. Pride is *self*-love. Pride declares: "I will make my own rules for right and wrong—I will decide what I will or won't do!" I will be autonomous. I will be my own creation and in effect, I will be god of my life!

Infected with pride, perhaps the man and woman now think the reason God has forbidden them the fruit is so they will remain below him. How could something that *looks* good bring death? As the Tempter urges them to deepen their "looking" at the forbidden tree he utters: "Surely you won't die!" God and his mission for humanity is being challenged not just in the heavens, but in the very physical order of creation and the hearts of man and woman.

This strategy works. They see the fruit as beautiful and good for eating. The Tempter rejoices. A *desire* has been created where one *never existed* previously. Something completely unnecessary for human happiness, peace, and fulfillment suddenly becomes a "need." The hearts of Adam and Eve turn from God to the new voice as the source of life and happiness. But in fact, turning closer to the voice of the Tempter is also a turning toward themselves as the source of happiness apart from God and a mission apart from God's mission. In this *seeing anew* and the new desires and needs it creates, lust, the spirit of *unchastity*, enters human history.

Think of children taunting a playmate to try something forbidden, saying, "It is not going to kill you" or, "It is fun!" "And besides, you're not going to be a mamma's girl and do everything you are told, are you?" Or think of when you wanted to experiment or to see *for yourself* whether you had been missing fun things. Don't you remember wondering in your heart whether *it* (whatever it was) was really as bad as you had been told?

---

[29] Can you remember the first time that you violated a command of your parents and were overcome with guild or remorse? Do you remember it as a scary choice or an exciting choice? Remember and get in touch with the history of our own conscience formation.

If the one tempted succumbs to the new desire or lust that has been created, experimentation to test *it*, and the pleasure *it* promises, must proceed. When any new lust is created, the allure and desire to experiment is overwhelming. At this point in the temptation, Adam and Eve no longer see God's plan as the only possible mission in life. They have heard new voices. Perhaps they now think obedience is limiting and constraining. A new potential within them has been awakened and perhaps they are now thinking they should trust this strange and exciting instinct. Maybe the fruit could be very good.

They are experiencing the *freedom to choose* for oneself, apart from God, also brings with it a new sense of personal power. This new personal power is the experience the Tempter promised of being *like God*. It is a potent temptation. Opened to them is a world of possibilities that match the many new urgings so recently awakened in their hearts. From the spirit of disobedience to that of spiritual un-chastity, only one step remains to complete the cycle. To "take" what does not below to them.

## THIRD STAGE
*Adrift From God and Lusting to Take Forbidden Fruit*
*They Violate Covenant Poverty*

Temptation's climax moves the person from the realm of interior disobedience and lustful thoughts to the world of action. Mere possibilities turn into concrete choices. If the one tempted believes that a new, better reality might bring happiness, she must experiment to test the truthfulness of what the "inspiration" proposed. Adam and Eve thus complete the cycle of the first sin by experimenting and taking what does not belong to them. Taking what does not belong to us and what we do not need is a violation of poverty: for we are to find our riches, our meaning, and our mission in "every word that comes from the mouth of God."

The effects of their action are immediate and catastrophic. They see each other now through their own godlike vision - a vision where each of them, and not God, is at the center of their universes. No longer united heart and mind with God, they see each other's beauty not as God sees it, but as something to be used for personal gain or satisfaction. They hide their nakedness from each other. Not because God has made sex unclean, but because they are fearful their partner will see and know how the loss of innocence has corrupted the designs of the human heart. In their *new knowledge* acquired from the fruit of Good and Evil, the human person, made *in dignity, in the image and likeness of God*, has become an *object* – the center of his/her own universe and thus, a means to an end for personal satisfaction.

No longer loving each other perfectly in their God-given dignity, they have to hide. Disobedience, lust, and taking what does not belong to oneself have tainted their relationship (mission) with each other, with God, and from this point forward, every relationship in human history will be scarred to greater or lesser degrees. Man and woman no longer live fully for God but now for themselves. This indeed is a very new mission for humanity: to serve the desires of human pride and not God. The human heart is forever divided. Greed, jealousy, anger, avarice, pride, and all other vices enter history and wreak havoc. And by severing their perfect union with God, paradise is forever lost.

*The Legacy of Sin - Excitement Followed by Loss*

What Genesis has detailed in the threefold sin of Adam and Eve is the blueprint of every single sin of every person in all of human history. Listen closely to your experience and you will be able to trace the three parts of *listening with new ears, seeing differently,* and *acting to test and experiment* in all your sinful acts. The first stage is marked by dividing our hearts by disobeying the voice of God in our conscience. The second stage builds on this initial disobedience and engenders new "freedoms" and their related lusts. And the third stage is to "test for myself" if I will indeed "die" by satisfying the lust. Here, we take what does not belong to us and what we really don't need, violating poverty.

How do we account for the excitement that accompanies sinful acts? Doesn't the excitement indicate we are on to some positive human good? There is a genuine excitement in becoming the center of my own universe - of stepping out into the "new" experiences of life. Not unlike the prodigal son who was lured by the promise of leaving his home and experimenting in a foreign land.

*"A man had two sons, and the younger son said to his father, 'Father, give me the share of your estate that should come to me.' So the father divided the property between them. After a few days, the younger son collected all his belongings and set off to a distant country where he squandered his inheritance on a life of dissipation".* Lk 15:11-13.

However, if you listen closely to your heart, you will feel both excitement *and* fear commingled in sinful contemplation and experimentation. The rush of excitement tinged with fear in sinful acts is a combination of becoming your "own god," and yet consciously or unconsciously knowing that you are violating the very commandments of the One, True God. It is impossible to contemplate sinful actions or to sin and not feel fear and anxiety. This is so because sin at its core severs our hearts and wills from God. Such actions for those made in God's image must by their very nature, engender fear and trembling.

When an individual frequently chooses against God in favor for the self, the conscience is silenced—buried. When this happens, one no longer "feels" the fear because one is spiritually dead and cut off from a life of grace.

*The Original Sin Gives Birth to the Enemy of Human Nature's Plan for a Unholy Diversity*

This one action of Adam and Eve, seemingly so insignificant, leads to the collapse of a sacred diversity; the holy communion of the relational world is shattered by self-love and the loss of innocence. In its place is a new world where every relationship is corrupted by self-love and the desire to build a kingdom or a paradise apart from God is doomed to failure. Sickness and death enter human history. Truly, innocence and paradise is lost!

It is this truth of a world divided by pride and self-love that St Augustine powerfully lays open to us in his masterwork, *The City of God*. Every attempt to bring union and communion to the human community—to make the diverse persons of the earth one—will be for not.[30] From this point forward, a battle will ensure between a unified sacred diversity and an individualistic unholy diversity.

In the loss of God as the center of the human heart, history's evolution will become one of coercive powers seeking to dominate others and subdue and enslave them. We will witness this in Scripture in the enslavement of the people of Israel in Egypt and God's subsequent act to free them from slavery.

As the true allegory of Genesis unfolds after this tragic choice, we witness the inauguration of a world with self-interest, not God, at the center of human desiring and choosing. In this loss of innocence and obedience to God, the woman and the man are ashamed to discover a desire to use the other for self-pleasure and they cover themselves to mask their profane desires. In this turn to self, the holy diversity of persons, male and female and made in God's image and likeness, is broken. The foundational relationship in all of human society—between man and woman called to "be fruitful and multiply" is wounded in the choice to turn from communion with God.

Labor by the sweat of one's brow, pain in childbirth and the subjugation of the powerful over the weak enters the relational world—and so does death and the loss of immortality.

---

[30] "The desire of the world-wide unity which fills the heart: of man will, in all likelihood, never die. Since the time it was proffered to them, even though in a mystical sense and on a supernatural level, it has never been forgotten. Generation after generation has honestly attempted to gather all men within the walls of an earthly city modeled upon the heavenly Jerusalem. They have studied everything except the Christian faith in order to find a common bond, but they have met with failure. Perhaps the time is ripe to recall the age-old metaphysical principle that only force capable of preserving a thing is the force which created it. It is completely useless to pursue a Christian end except by Christian means. If we really want one world, we must first have one church, and the only Church that is one is the Catholic Church.

Had we religious unity, we could peacefully enjoy all the other unities. Basically there is nothing wrong in attempting to achieve philosophical unity by philosophical means, nor in trying to establish world unity through philosophical unity. Philosophy really is a unifying force, as are science, art, industry and economic forces. There is no single factor in human unity that we can afford to despise. But, just as every physical undertaking is doomed to failure if secondary principles replace those which are primary, so also all efforts to unify mankind are bound to fail if the sole principle of unification is overlooked, especially when that principle is the unifying force of all the others. Philosophy, science, art and economics all can help in achieving the great work of mankind, but neither individually nor collectively is in their power to accomplish it. The besetting sin of all such undertakings is in the fact that they attempt, without Christ, to fulfill the promise made by Christ to men.

Such an achievement is quite impossible. It is conceivable that a number of men, more or less large, be unified under the domination of other men or even of one individual; however, if we are striving toward the unity of all men, we must look beyond mankind for that unifying principle. The only possible source of future unity lies not in multiplicity, but above it. One World is impossible without One God and One Church. In this truth lies the every timely message conveyed to man by St. Augustine's City of God." From Etienne Gilson's introduction to the City of God: Bourke, Vernon J., Doubleday/Image Books 1958. P 34-35.

*To the woman he said: I will intensify your toil in childbearing; in pain you shall bring forth children. Yet your urge shall be for your husband, and he shall rule over you. To the man he said: Because you listened to your wife and ate from the tree about which I commanded you, you shall not eat from it, Cursed is the ground because of you! In toil you shall eat its yield all the days of your life. Thorns and thistles it shall bear for you, and you shall eat the grass of the field. By the sweat of your brow you shall eat bread, until you return to the ground, from which you were taken; For you are dust, and to dust you shall return. (Gn 3: 16-19)*

We witness the unfolding of the true allegory of the world after the fall from communion with God in the story of fratricide of Cain for Abel.

*Cain said to his brother Abel, "Let us go out in the field." When they were in the field, Cain attacked his brother Abel and killed him. (Gn 4:8)*

We see corruption in human society and the destruction unfold in the great flood.

*When the LORD saw how great the wickedness of human beings was on earth, and how every desire that their heart conceived was always nothing but evil, the LORD regretted making human beings on the earth, and his heart was grieved. (Gn 6: 5-6)*

And the holy diversity of all persons once at one with God is symbolized in the Tower of Babel's profane diversity of individuals cut off from God and each other and unable to achieve human progress.

*The whole world had the same language and the same words. When they were migrating from the east, they came to a valley in the land of Shinar and settled there. They said to one another, "Come, let us mold bricks and harden them with fire." They used bricks for stone, and bitumen for mortar. Then they said, "Come, let us build ourselves a city and a tower with its top in the sky and so make a name for ourselves; otherwise we shall be scattered all over the earth." The LORD came down to see the city and the tower that the people had built. Then the LORD said: If now, while they are one people and all have the same language, they have started to do this, nothing they presume to do will be out of their reach. Come, let us go down and there confuse their language, so that no one will understand the speech of another. So the LORD scattered them from there over all the earth, and they stopped building the city. That is why it was called Babel, because there the LORD confused the speech of all the world. From there the LORD scattered them over all the earth. (Gn 11: 1-9).*

One sinful experiment can lead to another and another until a person, a people, a race, a nation, are more and more cut off from God's life and mission. Both the individual and the corporate conscience are darkened, no longer seeing distinctions between good and evil. The mission to serve self seems more real and attractive - a greater positive human good - than to be obedient to the voice of God in our hearts. It becomes very hard even to hear God's voice in our hearts.

The legacy of the divided human heart and the rejection of full communion with God reverberates throughout all of human history. It is even manifest in the human members of the Church. Our sinfulness harms the body of Christ and the Church, marring the unity that God desires. God will prevail, however, even over the sinfulness of Christians, because Jesus' passion, death, and resurrection have forever broken the tragic legacy of sin.

Listen to how sin works in your life. Try to trace the threefold patterns of listening, seeing, and acting - disobedience, lust, and greed. How are you tempted to be your own god? What issues and choices most appeal to your ego so that making your *own* decisions over and above God's authority gives you a sense of being your *own* person?

It may be helpful to think of sin as a tree with roots, a trunk, branches, and fruit. See your individual sins as fruit on a tree. Tracing back from the fruit to the branches to the trunk to the roots, pray for the grace to understand the *root* sins in your life. While all sinful fruit manifests characteristics of the seven capital sins (pride, anger, envy, greed, lust, avarice, laziness), the *trunk* and *root* sin in our lives will most likely be localized in one or other of these - pride is almost always present because the first sin appealed to human pride and independence from God.

Many people have a hard time understanding sin and how it works in their lives. Many also lack an understanding of the two great spiritual forces outside of themselves, each seeking to engage us in a different mission. St. Ignatius, in his *Spiritual Exercises*, calls these two missions *the two standards*. Christ's standard is one of poverty, humility, and bearing the ridicule of the world in order to bring about the Father's kingdom. Satan's standard celebrates the riches of the world, and the honors and pride that makes man, not God, the center of the human project.

Most people know they do things that are wrong, but they lack the understanding of why they do the things they do or how the temptation to act wrongly fits into these two missions or standards described above. Let me present a short reflection on how human sinfulness entered the world (and still enters it through our choices and actions). It will help you be present to your experience with an amazing new awareness of how grace and sin work in your life and how the spirit of God and the spirit of darkness operate.

First, God has a plan and a mission for you. God's loving plan for us as individuals and as his people is not random or governed by chance. It is deliberate and one might even say, strategic. Creation and salvation history have nothing to do with chaos theory. God wants your heart, and he uses love to get your attention. He wants you actively engaged in the mission of the Son in the world. God is purposeful and deliberate in his concern for you. He knows your strengths and the love in your heart and how to move you to choose the option of life. He never wastes an opportunity to confront you with love, peace, and mercy to help you understand your life and the mission of love you are destined to share with Jesus.

It is also important to understand that the Tempter's plan is also deliberate, purposeful, and strategic. He also wants you to share in a mission. Understanding how temptation works and how we fall under its spell is an important step in any person's faith life. The Tempter has a plan to separate you from God. He knows your weaknesses and how to trap you and he, likewise, never wastes an opportunity.

If you think of the Tempter as deliberately "playing you" to lead you away from joy, peace, and love, you will have an accurate picture of his intent and purposes. Also, by paying attention to the strategic nature of temptation and the mission you are being seduced to share, you will not dead-end in guilt when examining your life. Instead, you will tend to focus more on how you have fallen prey to the one who seeks your destruction and misery. This knowledge will help you always turn in hope to God, who can rescue you from the "snares of the fowler."

The Tempter is effective largely because he poses options to our confused consciences that "seem" to open the way to life, excitement, and new possibilities for growth. He presents a mission that seems positive. However, as choices and options that promise pleasure, they never, absolutely never, end up pleasurable, never lead us to growth and new life. The initial promise of excitement ends in a deadened spirit. St. Ignatius reminds us in his rules for discerning the different spirits, that the angel of darkness often masquerades as an angel of light to cover his tracks. Here, in the true, mythic verse of Scripture, is how it all began.

# Chapter Two

## GOD CALLS US TO COME HOME FOR THE JOY OF RECONCILIATION

*Coming Home - the Joy of Reconciliation*

The call for persons to return to full relationship with God is present in the very early history of the Judeo-Christian faith. The ancient Jewish custom having the heart of the morning and evening prayer begin with what is called the *Shema*—"*Hear O Israel*"—in Deuteronomy 6:4:

> *Hear, O Israel! The LORD is our God, the LORD alone!*

The commandment to re-establish an exclusive relationship with the Creator and to love and listen to His voice alone continues in Deut. verses 5-9:

> *Therefore, you shall love the LORD, your God, with your whole heart, and with your whole being, and with your whole strength. Take to heart these words which I command you today. Keep repeating them to your children. Recite them when you are at home and when you are away, when you lie down and when you get up. Bind them on your arm as a sign- and let them be as a pendant on your forehead. Write them on the doorposts of your houses and on your gates.*

Israel is presented with the choice—the mission—to follow God. To listen, love, and obey God leads to life. To refuse to listen, love and obey, leads to death. We read later in Deuteronomy 30: 15-20:

> *See, I have today set before you life and good, death and evil. If you obey the commandments of the LORD, your God, which I am giving you today, loving the LORD, your God, and walking in his ways, and keeping his commandments, statutes and ordinances, you will live and grow numerous, and the LORD, your God, Will bless you in the land you are entering to possess. If, however, your heart turns away and you do not obey, but are led astray and bow down to other gods and serve them, I tell you today that you will certainly perish; you will not have a long life on the land which you are crossing the Jordan to enter and possess. I call heaven and earth today to witness against you: I have set before you life and death, the blessing and the curse.*
> 
> ***Choose life, then, that you and your descendants may live, By Loving the LORD, your God, Obeying his voice, And Holding fast to him.***
> 
> *For that will mean life for you, a long life for you to live on the land which the LORD swore to your ancestors, To Abraham, Isaac, and Jacob, to give to them.*

And moving forward to the New Testament, Christ affirms the central "relationship" requirements for people to bring order and peace back into human history:

> When the Pharisees heard that he had silenced the Sadducees, they gathered together, and one of them [a scholar of the law] tested him by asking, "Teacher, which commandment in the law is the greatest?" He said to him, "You shall love the Lord, your God, with all your heart, with all your soul, and with all your mind. This is the greatest and the first commandment. The second is like it: You shall love your neighbor as yourself. The whole law and the prophets depend on these two commandments." *Matthew 22: 34-40*

This holy vocation for Israel to reestablish relationship with God is actually God's work in human history. From the moment of the fall, God had a plan to weave the shattered unity of humanity back into one people. This is movingly and beautifully rendered in the famous 1432 panel painting of the Annunciation by the Renaissance master, Fra Angelico. In the image we see off to the left Adam and Eve being banished from Paradise with the rays of the Holy Spirit of God extending from the tragic moment to the annunciation by Gabriel to the Blessed Mother of the Christ child to be born of her.

We remember at this point that most famous of all Gospel passages that you see on placards at every national sporting event -- JOHN 3:16:

> *For God so loved the world that he gave his only Son, so that everyone who believes in him might not perish but might have eternal life.*

God's work in Christ was to reunify creation and human nature made in God's image and likeness. The whole of creation and the locus of its renewal in the Church, as Pope Francis has reminded us recently, is a love story. "We, the women and men of the Church, we are in the middle of a love story: each of us is a link in this chain of love. And if we do not understand this, we have understood nothing of what the Church is."[31]

The first gift Christ gives the Church for the reunification of all relationships in God is baptism.[32] But because our human nature has been wounded by sin, the power of baptism must be renewed constantly by grace in the

---

[31] The Church is not merely "a human enterprise," but rather "a love story," said Pope Francis, and the faithful must remember that it is only in the path of love that the Church can grow. The Church began "in the heart of the Father," said the Pope at an April 24 Mass for Vatican Bank employees in the Chapel of the Casa Santa Marta. "So this love story began, a story that has gone on for so long, and is not yet ended," he explained. "We, the women and men of the Church, we are in the middle of a love story: each of us is a link in this chain of love. And if we do not understand this, we have understood nothing of what the Church is." Pointing to the growth and persecution of the early Church, Pope Francis stressed that the faithful must not compromise to get "more partners in this enterprise," Vatican Radio reported. He cautioned that "the Church does not grow by human strength" but through the path of love. While some Christians have "taken the wrong path" and "waged wars of religion," he said, "that is not the story of love." "Yet we learn, with our mistakes, how the story of love goes," he continued, explaining that it is the Holy Spirit rather than any military strength that allows the Church to grow. The Pontiff asked the mothers in the congregation how they might feel if someone referred to them as "a domestic administrator." He suggested that they might respond, "No, I am the mother!" Likewise, he said, "the Church is Mother." "And we are in the middle of a love story that continues thanks to the power of the Holy Spirit. All of us together are a family in the Church, who is our Mother," he explained. Pope Francis turned to Mary to ask for "the grace of the spiritual joy of participating in this love story" with her son." Excerpt from homily of Pope Francis at Casa Santa Marta; 4-24-13.

[32] Although it is proper to each individual, original sin does not have the character of a personal fault in any of Adam's descendants. It is a deprivation of original holiness and justice, but human nature has not been totally corrupted: it is wounded in the natural powers proper to it, subject to ignorance, suffering and the dominion of death, and inclined to sin - an inclination to evil that is called concupiscence". Baptism, by

sacrament of reconciliation.³³ The mercy of God is infinite for those banished from paradise and wounded by sin. There is simply no limit to God's mercy and we therefore must never tire in asking God for forgiveness.

It is also why we must not rewrite the laws of human nature to normalize our fallen condition. There are many temptations to do this and all of them seek their inspiration, wittingly or unwitting, from the Original Sin to separate our nature from God and seek to re-write creation in our own image.

This is why Jesus seeks to portray the love of God the Church must model in the person of the father in the story of the prodigal son. The prodigal son came home to satisfy his most basic needs for food. Perhaps expecting to be treated at best as hired help, he had given up hope of having the love and friendship that makes a real home. After all, he betrayed his father, his family name, his people, and his religion.

But Jesus clearly intends us to understand the father's response to the lost son as God's response to all sinners who are lost and seek reconciliation. We expect to be punished in some way because of our violations. But in the father's response, Jesus portrays a love and mercy that knows no limits, even in the face of sinfulness that knew no limits. Far from being punished, the father celebrates and gives the boy a signet ring symbolizing his reinstatement as a son with all family privileges.

The sacrament of reconciliation is the pathway back home to paradise and to the active participation in God's mission. For this reason, it is a prayer of joy and a real missionary activity. The more profoundly we are in touch with our sinfulness, the deeper our joy becomes when we surrender our sin and weakness to Jesus and surrender anew to his mission and kingdom. In reconciliation we are, through the power and mercy of God, reclaiming our lost home, our original mission, and the paradise of peace and joy God always intended us to share.

> *Blessed be the God and Father of our Lord Jesus Christ, who in his great mercy gave us a new birth to a living hope through the resurrection of Jesus Christ from the dead, to an inheritance that is imperishable, undefiled, and unfading, kept in heaven for you who by the power of God are safeguarded through faith, to a salvation that is ready to be revealed in the final time. In this you rejoice, although now for a little while you may have to suffer through various trials, so that the genuineness of your faith, more precious than gold that is perishable even though tested by*

---

imparting the life of Christ's grace, erases original sin and turns a man back towards God, but the consequences for nature, weakened and inclined to evil, persist in man and summon him to spiritual battle. CCC #405. Our Lord tied the forgiveness of sins to faith and Baptism: "Go into all the world and preach the gospel to the whole creation. He who believes and is baptized will be saved."⁵²¹ Baptism is the first and chief sacrament of forgiveness of sins because it unites us with Christ, who died for our sins and rose for our justification, so that "we too might walk in newness of life." CCC #977.

³³ "When we made our first profession of faith while receiving the holy Baptism that cleansed us, the forgiveness we received then was so full and complete that there remained in us absolutely nothing left to efface, neither original sin nor offenses committed by our own will, nor was there left any penalty to suffer in order to expiate them. . . . Yet the grace of Baptism delivers no one from all the weakness of nature. On the contrary, we must still combat the movements of concupiscence that never cease leading us into evil." CCC # 978.

> *fire, may prove to be for praise, glory, and honor at the revelation of Jesus Christ. Although you have not seen him you love him; even though you do not see him now yet believe in him, you rejoice with an indescribable and glorious joy, as you attain the goal of your faith, the salvation of your souls. 1 Pt 1:3-9*

St. Ignatius considers it a grace to know our sinfulness, for in knowing it, we come to realize that we need Jesus as Redeemer. It is the Tempter that makes us feel we cannot go home or that we won't be forgiven. Never forget the lessons of the prodigal son. God will never turn you away, no matter what your sins. If you feel fear, realize it is coming from the one who wants you to lose hope in ever being able to go home or to start over. Fear and loss of hope play big parts in the Tempter's *strategy* to keep us "lost" and tethered to his mission.

*The Joy of Reconciliation Is Both Yours and the Lord's*

Jesus died to save you *from* eternal loss and *for* eternal life and to reclaim human history and creation for the Creator. He did this out of love for you. I believe that Jesus would have suffered and died to save just one lost soul, he loves us individually that much. Give Jesus the joy of knowing that his sacrifice for you is bearing fruit for he wants to become one with you and give restore your eternal life. Listen to these words taken from the Divine Office for Holy Saturday that the Church gives us each year on the most significant day of the liturgical calendar:

> *Rise, let us leave this place. The enemy led you out of the earthly paradise. I will not restore you to that paradise, but I will enthrone you in heaven. I forbade you the tree that was only a symbol of life, but see, I who am life itself am now one with you. I appointed cherubim to guard you as slaves are guarded, but now I make them worship you as God.*

Give him the joy of confessing your sinfulness and letting him forgive you and start you once again on the mission that gives your life meaning and hope. You can give Jesus, the Good Shepherd, no greater gift. He loves us in our weakness and sinfulness and *never* judges harshly the one who genuinely seeks his forgiveness.

Before Christ's atoning death, *no one* had the hope of eternal life with God. Jesus' death has won our reconciliation. When we express sorrow for our sinfulness and seek God's forgiveness, we are healed and grow in the perfection won for us by Christ. In confessing and being pardoned, we have the sure hope of gaining eternal life. Nothing can bring us more joy. Nothing can bring Jesus more joy than our taking seriously his ultimate gift of reconciling love.

The reception of the sacrament of reconciliation on a regular basis is the indispensable way to constantly renew and deepen our relationship with God. It also strengthens us on our own mission to cooperate with Christ in his work of universal reconciliation for God's kingdom. For this reason, we should think of it not just as a pathway to God but as an essential form of prayer. Frequent reception of the sacrament will significantly increase your joy, happiness, and peace. It will continue the healing of all your relationships.

The Second Vatican Council calls the sacrament of reconciliation the second most important means toward growth in holiness. The first is the Eucharist. Since the Church is in the business of producing a holy, missionary people for the purpose of transforming the world in the image of Christ, it is no wonder she would be interested in promoting this gift of healing and joy. John Paul II, in his address for the World Day of Peace for 2002, said that there is no peace in the world without justice and no justice without forgiveness. The personal path toward that peace, justice, and forgiveness of which he speaks begins for each Catholic in this great sacrament of healing.

Barring serious sin, we are asked to receive this sacrament only once a year. I am constantly amazed at how little is asked of us in our faith commitment. You may want to consider a frequency that is closer to once a month. I think the Holy Father goes weekly. Frequent reception on a monthly basis will do more than you can possibly imagine in helping you grow in faith and closeness to God and in self-awareness of your own mission in life.

The subjects in the three categories mentioned below are ways we can fall into temptation and follow the mission of the Tempter. These different categories are helpful reflections to keep us alert to God's mission and where we often need Jesus' reconciling love to get back on track in our lives. Take your time in praying over your life. Pray to understand the patterns of temptation to which you are susceptible. Pray to God to know where you need the forgiveness of Jesus. Know that you are moving more deeply toward your true mission in life. Your efforts to grow in this way bring joy not only to your heart but also to Jesus'. Make the sacrament of reconciliation a regular part of the mission of your spiritual life.

Also, notice how a traditional preparation for confession or an "examination of conscience" focuses on the "relational dimension" of life. We traditionally focus on our relationship with God, our "self" and "others" when we are preparing for Reconciliation. Here is an example:

*In My Relationship with God...*

✠ Do I take the time to make this relationship one that is real and vital, with a life of prayer and thanksgiving?
✠ Have I considered religious preoccupations foolish, peripheral, or of no consequence in my life?
✠ Do I skip Sunday Mass for the sake of convenience? Am I aware that to do so is a grave sin?
✠ Do I receive the Lord in communion without going to confession when I have consciously committed some grave sin like missing Mass on Sunday or a holy day or engaging in sexual intercourse outside of marriage?

- Do I regularly doubt God's love for other people or myself?
- Do I receive the sacrament of reconciliation at least once a year to gain the grace of forgiveness?
- Do I make up my own rules for right and wrong, and discard the teachings of the Gospel and the Church when they begin to press upon my own life?
- Do I profane God's holy name by using Jesus or God as a swear word?

### *In Relationship to My Own Life...*

- Do I live for ease and comfort: for "self" alone?
- Have I lacked gratitude for the basic blessings of life, health, and friends?
- Do I allow power or money to control my plans and relationships? This is idolatry, worshipping a god other than God.
- Have I failed to cultivate my natural talents?
- Have I abused my body and/ or health?
- Do I abuse alcohol or drugs?
- Do I use or purchase pornography from magazines, movies or the Internet?
- Do I speak up about my beliefs and convictions in appropriate ways in public settings, or do I let my fear of rejection silence me?
- Do I rationalize sinful behavior instead of allowing myself to be challenged to face the responsibility of my actions?
- Have I had an abortion?

### *In My Relationships with Others...*

- Do I treat my parents, family and friends with respect and love?
- Have I rejected the love or friendship of another?
- Have I failed to share what I am able to share in goods or services with the poor and needy?
- Have I harmed another's reputation by gossip or malicious talk?
- Have I failed to forgive certain people?
- Do I hold onto anger? Am I envious of others?
- Do I hold sacred and reserve sexual intimacy for marriage? (This is not a law made up by the Church, but a command of Christ himself that the Church has a responsibility to proclaim as Jesus' Way, Truth and Life).
- Have I assisted another in getting an abortion?
- Have I tried to control others for my own personal satisfaction or have I been cruel, hateful, or self-centered in dealing with individuals or groups?
- Have I been faithful to friends who need my help or support?
- Am I truthful in my use of money and in business? Have I lied? Have I cheated on exams or papers?
- Have I stolen money or possessions from others?

*The Eucharist is our Communion with God in the Blood of Christ*

Baptism and reconciliation are sacraments designed to heal our relationship with God, to repair our wounded human nature and grant us the grace to treat others as God has treated us. And the most important sacrament for our relationship with God is the Holy Eucharist. It is indeed a Communion "in spirit and truth" with God in Christ and through Christ with all of God's creation.

Of this new world that the God is creating by virtue of Jesus birth, death and resurrection, it will be accomplished by the Christ's church. It is the Church that the Lord will use to re-weave humanity back into one body and this is why the sacrament of the Body and Blood of Christ is so essential for this universal work of reconciliation of the entire cosmos. We do well to recall that the word "liturgy" in the original Greek connotes a public service done on the part of one for the many. This of course, is what Christ does for us in the Holy Eucharist Liturgy. It is a work whereby he will reunite all of creation for those who follow the voice of God in Christ. We read of this Sacred Liturgy in the moving words of the Second Vatican Council and its role in bringing all things back into God's life in Christ. The selection below is also part of the annual cycle of readings in the Church's Divine Office. And appropriately enough, it is from the second Saturday after Easter. It is important enough to include this section from the Council's documents for our reflection:

*God who "wills that all men be saved and come to the knowledge of the truth" (1 Tim. 2:4), "who in many and various ways spoke in times past to the fathers by the prophets" (Heb. 1:1), when the fullness of time had come sent His Son, the Word made flesh, anointed by the Holy Spirit, to preach the gospel to the poor, to heal the contrite of heart, to be a "bodily and spiritual medicine", the Mediator between God and man. For His humanity, united with the person of the Word, was the instrument of our salvation. Therefore in Christ "the perfect achievement of our reconciliation came forth, and the fullness of divine worship was given to us". The wonderful works of God among the people of the Old Testament were but a prelude to the work of Christ the Lord in redeeming mankind and giving perfect glory to God. He achieved His task principally by the paschal mystery of His blessed passions resurrection from the dead, and the glorious ascension, whereby "dying, he destroyed our death and, rising, he restored our life". For it was from the side of Christ as He slept the sleep of death upon the cross that there came forth "the wondrous sacrament of the whole Church".*

*Just as Christ was sent by the Father, so also He sent the apostles, filled with the Holy Spirit. This He did that, by preaching the gospel to every creature, they might proclaim that the Son of God, by His death and resurrection, had freed us from the power of Satan and from death, and brought us into the kingdom of His Father. His purpose also was that they might accomplish the work of salvation which they had proclaimed, by means of sacrifice and sacraments, around which the entire liturgical life revolves. Thus by baptism men are plunged into the paschal mystery of Christ: they die with Him, are buried with Him, and rise with Him; they receive the spirit of adoption as sons "in which we cry: Abba, Father" (Rom. 8:15), and thus become true adorers whom the Father seeks. In like manner, as often as they eat the supper of the Lord they proclaim the death of the Lord until He comes. For that reason, on the very day of Pentecost, when the Church appeared before the world, "those who received the word" of Peter "were baptized." And "they continued steadfastly in the teaching of the apostles*

> and in the communion of the breaking of bread and in prayers . . . praising God and being in favor with all the people" (Acts 2:41-47). From that time onwards the Church has never failed to come together to celebrate the paschal mystery: reading those things "which were in all the scriptures concerning him" (Luke 24:27), celebrating the eucharist in which "the victory and triumph of his death are again made present", and at the same time giving thanks "to God for his unspeakable gift" (2 Cor. 9:15) in Christ Jesus, "in praise of his glory" (Eph. 1:12), through the power of the Holy Spirit.[34]

God choose the people of Israel to prepare the world for the Messiah who would heal all relationships and bring about the "new heavens and the new earth." It will be the Church of Christ that is to be the vessel whereby God will bring about the New Jerusalem and the new unity of all in him due to his "labor of love" in the passion and crucifixion. The selection below is appropriately placed on the very last Friday of the liturgical year before the commencement of Advent:

> Then I saw a new heaven and a new earth. The former heaven and the former earth had passed away, and the sea was no more. I also saw the holy city, a new Jerusalem, coming down out of heaven from God, prepared as a bride adorned for her husband. I heard a loud voice from the throne saying, "Behold, God's dwelling is with the human race. He will dwell with them and they will be his people and God himself will always be with them [as their God]. He will wipe every tear from their eyes, and there shall be no more death or mourning, wailing or pain, [for] the old order has passed away." The one who sat on the throne said, "Behold, I make all things new." Then he said, "Write these words down, for they are trustworthy and true." He said to me, "They are accomplished. I [am] the Alpha and the Omega, the beginning and the end. To the thirsty I will give a gift from the spring of life-giving water. The victor will inherit these gifts, and I shall be his God, and he will be my son. But as for cowards, the unfaithful, the depraved, murderers, the unchaste, sorcerers, idol-worshipers, and deceivers of every sort, their lot is in the burning pool of fire and sulfur, which is the second death." RV 21: 1-8.

It is the unity of the Body of Christ in the Church, which is to be the sign and symbol of Christ's unifying redemption work on the part of all creation. This New Jerusalem which will only become fully realized at the second coming of Christ is already at work due to his Spirit in the Church. We no longer live under the law of the Old Covenant but under the new law of Love in Christ Jesus:

> But now that faith has come, we are no longer under a disciplinarian. For through faith you are all children of God* in Christ Jesus. For all of you who were baptized into Christ have clothed yourselves with Christ. There is neither Jew nor Greek, there is neither slave nor free person,

---

[34] Vatican Council II: *Sacrosanctum Concilium*, Chapter I [1] 5.

*there is not male and female; for you are all one in Christ Jesus. And if you belong to Christ, then you are Abraham's descendant, heirs according to the promise.* GAL 3:25-9.

We must be aware how significant is the call to unity in the Body of Christ. For the subtle temptations of the enemy of human nature who seeks to destroy all relationships can even be present—perhaps most especially present—in the Church. This is why we hear of Jesus harsh condemnations of the scribes and the Pharisees who accused him of calling on the power of Satan to perform his might works.

*Then they brought to him a demoniac who was blind and mute. He cured the mute person so that he could speak and see. All the crowd was astounded, and said, "Could this perhaps be the Son of David?" But when the Pharisees heard this, they said, "This man drives out demons only by the power of Beelzebul, the prince of demons." But he knew what they were thinking and said to them,* "*Every kingdom divided against itself will be laid waste, and no town or house divided against itself will stand. And if Satan drives out Satan, he is divided against himself; how, then, will his kingdom stand? And if I drive out demons by Beelzebul, by whom do your own people* drive them out? Therefore they will be your judges. But if it is by the Spirit of God that I drive out demons, then the kingdom of God has come upon you. How can anyone enter a strong man's house and steal his property, unless he first ties up the strong man? Then he can plunder his house. Whoever is not with me is against me, and whoever does not gather with me scatters. Therefore, I say to you, every sin and blasphemy will be forgiven people, but blasphemy against the Spirit* will not be forgiven. And whoever speaks a word against the Son of Man will be forgiven; but whoever speaks against the holy Spirit will not be forgiven, either in this age or in the age to come.* Mt 12: 22-32.

# Chapter Three

## A SHORT COURSE ON SPIRITUAL DISCERNMENT

Part One: Entering the School of Discernment

The biblical account of paradise in Genesis not only presents the scriptural starting point for human history, it also provides an opening to understand our life as a sacred story. Many incorrectly imagine Adam and Eve's fall as the beginning of our story. But the Book of Genesis begins with our first parents in perfect relationship with God, for we were created in God's own image, who is Love.

Our hope in reading this section is that you will enter a "school of discernment." You will be invited to see God, others and the world around you in light of the perfect relationship that existed at the beginning of human history.

More than that, you will be invited to begin the "Sacred Story" prayer, a spiritual discipline where God can begin to work his miracle of healing, forgiveness and hope within you and the students whom you teach, to continue the work of healing your life and your relationship to God, to others and creation.

*Perfect relationship*

Spiritual discernment is challenging. Because of the fall — original sin — we do not easily distinguish truth from falsehood. As a result, we fall short of understanding God and the gift God gives in creation.

The relationship of love shared by the three persons of the Trinity is the model of the perfect relationship of eternal love God intended for our first parents. When they severed their relationship with Love, blame, grief and death entered our story and all our relationships.
We are heirs to this original sin of broken relationships and so inherit their vulnerability to sickness, disease, fear of abandonment and loneliness. But God's work in creation cannot be undone by sin. Out of this tragedy, God is able to create an even more astonishing good.

Christ waits for you to accept his invitation to participate in his grand work of reconciliation. You do this by opening to life as sacred story.

Your discernment will be easier if you imagine everything in light of the perfect relationships God intended, and the tragedy of broken relationships our first parents, as embodied spirits, introduced into our stories in rejecting Love. The perfect relationship was given and lost, but it is being restored in Christ. Entering this mystery of creation, iniquity and redemption will be our task and our goal over the next "forty weeks."

*School of discernment*

Every thought, word and deed that affirms the truth of perfect relationship and the human nature willed by God, and every effort to heal damaged relationships, is a work of the divine-inspirer; God the creator.

Every thought, word and deed that alters the truth of perfect relationship and the human nature willed by God, and everything that further undermines damaged relationships, is a work of the counter-inspirer; "the enemy of human nature," who from the beginning, is a murderer and a liar — the father of lies. (Jn 8: 43-45)

As you enter the school of spiritual discernment over the next year, keep your heart and mind focused on what I call the relational paradigm. You will be seeking the knowledge of your identity as a child of God informed by the truth of perfect relationship.
Your authentic identity is a human nature, willed by God. It is the unity of body and spirit. You will be seeking the knowledge of your authentic God-given human nature as it has been violated and broken by original sin.

And you will be seeking this knowledge in light of what Christ is offering you by his life, death and resurrection: the full healing that will be completed in the world and the life to come.

In short, you will be seeking the knowledge of perfect relationship and how in your own life and the world, that perfection has been broken but can also be restored, healed and redeemed by the divine physician. You will also be seeking knowledge of the thief and the robber — the enemy of human nature — who seeks to distort what authentic relationship is, and to hide from you the truth of God and your authentic human nature.

Sacred Story prayer invites you to discern the two plot-lines in your life: the one that leads to curse and death and the one that leads to life and blessings. Ultimately, you are seeking to know truth from falsehood in all of your thoughts, words and deeds.

What do you need for the journey? A generous heart and a willingness to be transformed by Christ's purifying forgiveness and mercy.

*Reflection*

In your own life history, how has your perfect relationship with God and with others been broken? What would you like Christ to heal? Ask for it!

*Instructions for the Journey*

Daily relationship with God in prayer is essential, and is best engaged in a true technology free zone. The recommended time for your prayer is 15 minutes—no more and no less.

*Prayer Exercises*

1. Commit yourself to praying daily for fifteen minutes over the next four weeks. Reflect on these materials during that time or pray with the Sacred Story Examen Prayer. A text version and an audio version can be found at [www.nwcatholic.org](www.nwcatholic.org).

2. For fifteen seconds after you awake and before you lie down for sleep, ask Jesus to burn away the selfishness and hardheartedness of sin's legacy in your history, and to transform it into a sacred story.

Part Two: Encountering the Spiritual World

In the previous selection we examined how our spirit, body and God's grace compose a holy trinity at work in us. All three parts working cooperatively are necessary for holiness and human growth.

In the paradise depicted in Genesis, the perfect cooperation of this trinity of human nature rendered us immortal. By turning from the fullness of God's grace, the perfect balance of the divinely crafted trinity was shattered and our immortality was lost. Now we turn our attention to Christ's incarnation and death, which reopened the way to immortality.

The Genesis account of our first parents is an allegory, a symbolic description of a real event that Catholic Church tradition calls the original sin. We will never know the exact context for the original sin or how the enemy of human nature tempted Adam and Eve to reject God and to make themselves "masters of their own universe."

Yet the Genesis account provides valuable clues for our reflection about temptation and the fall from grace that has evolved over time. It describes how God has been displaced from the center of human hearts and history.

*Two Voices*

By dissecting the story, we begin to understand how the spiritual world works. We discern the difference between the "voice" of God and the "voice" of the enemy of human nature. Learning to distinguish the difference between these two voices takes practice and, most importantly, it requires listening, time, trial and error, prayer, patience and God's grace.

The encounter with the spiritual world is an encounter with forces that support our growth and forces that want to disrupt our growth. Both forces have always been present in our life story, and our goal in last month's column, and the columns to follow over the next year, is to become conscious of these two plot lines; one that leads to blessing and life, and one that leads to curse and death.

Scripture and tradition teach us that God created our human nature as a unity of physical body and rational soul so God could be intimate with us. Complete intimacy with God is our destiny, our glory and the purpose of our creation.

Our first parents' human nature as physical bodies and spiritual souls was in complete harmony with God. We call this period of history "Paradise" or original justice. Original justice afforded our first parents complete self-mastery. They were at one in themselves, at one with each other and creation and at one with God.

The perfect harmony of Paradise is shattered when obedience, chastity and poverty are violated. Obedience is violated when we, like our first parents in the story of creation, make ourselves the final arbiters of truth and turning from God, follow our self-centered desires. This is the first stage of the original sin.

The second stage of the original sin commences when, cut off from God, we opened ourselves to illegitimate desires. Desires today deemed "objectively wrong" by the Commandments, the Gospel and tradition. In this, we violated chastity. "We decide" what we will and will not do.

Finally, we are moved to take what we do not need. In this third stage of the original sin, we experimented to finding out who was telling the truth, God or Lucifer.

In this experimenting, we violated poverty when we took what does not rightfully belong to us because now, "it's our life" and we will decide autonomous from God.

*Awakening to God's Voice*

Through his life, ministry, death and resurrection, Jesus reopens the way to immortality and complete harmony with God. When Jesus begins his public ministry, he confronts the triple sin of our first parents.

Lucifer tempts him to turn stones into bread, and he confronts the violation of poverty by refusing to take what is not offered him by the Father. (Mt 4:4) Next he deals with the violation of chastity and illegitimate desires by refusing to gain attention by plunging from the temple parapet. (Mt 4:7) Finally, he confronts the violation of obedience by refusing to serve Lucifer and rule on this earth. (Mt 4:10)

Sacred Story prayer journey challenges us to awaken to the voice of God in our own unique history, calling us to the poverty, chastity and obedience that can bring peace and repair sin's damage. To do this effectively, we will explore in future columns discernment guidelines modeled on St. Ignatius' classic Rules for spiritual discernment.

By understanding the Ignatian discernment guidelines, we can awaken more easily to our authentic human nature and identify and resist the illegitimate desires autonomy from God inspires. To prepare ourselves, we will learn a new language of discernment and discover how to distinguish the voice of God from the voice of the enemy of human nature in our thoughts, words and deeds.

*Reflection*

Can you identify how temptations against poverty, chastity and obedience play out in your story? Identify your main temptation in each vow and ask Christ for enlightenment, healing and forgiveness. Be specific and ask for help!

*Instructions for the journey*

The school of discernment requires spiritual exercise. Most importantly, it requires listening, time, trial and error, prayer (15 minutes each day), patience and God's grace.

*Prayer Exercises*

1. Commit yourself to praying daily over the next four weeks for 15 minutes — no more, no less. Ponder how the reflections in this column link to your own life story. You also may pray the Sacred Story Examen Prayer. A text version and an audio version can be found at **www.nwcatholic.org**.


Part Three: Reconciliation is the Goal of Spiritual Discernment

St. Ignatius lived for thirty years with his lower appetites in near complete control of his life. His awakening was guided by God and began while recuperating from an injury suffered in battle. During his recovery Ignatius was graced to notice a difference between two sets of fantasies or daydreams.

In the first fantasy, he imagined himself successful in marrying the daughter of Spain's King Ferdinand and Queen Isabella. He describes this later as a vain fantasy. In the second daydream, he imagines himself making a pilgrimage to Jerusalem and living like the saints.

Both daydreams made him feel good while he entertained them, but on deeper reflection, the afterglow of the first fantasy left him dry and dissatisfied while the afterglow of the second left him feeling content and peaceful.

With his awakening, the future saint began a life-long practice of spiritual discernment that transformed his life and the history of Christian spirituality.
In the first two reflections, we entered the school of discernment and described the encounter with the opposing forces of the spiritual world — one leading to blessing and life, one leading to curse and death.

These reflections awaken us to how sin confused the heart between a true and false identity and why discernment is now necessary for every one of us.

Before our first parents, by free choice, made themselves the center of their own universe — made *themselves* gods — spiritual discernment was not necessary. They knew the true God, they knew who they were and they knew instinctively how to act with integrity and holiness.

The biblical account of Adam and Eve recounts how humanity, listening to Satan's false promises, rejected God's voice as sole guide of the human conscience. Spiritual discernment is essential because this original sin—this primordial rupture from God—has forever divided our hearts. We easily confuse our selfish desires as life-giving and God's call to selfless love as life-threatening.

The Genesis account expresses the rupture that occurred between humankind and God. We cannot determine when in history this rupture took place, but our Judeo-Christian tradition affirms that it did occur, and history attests to its tragic consequences.

Corruption, disease and death entered our history when we lost the ability to instinctively know the truth about God, our human nature and creation. It is no wonder that the First Commandment states: "I am the Lord your God; you shall not have strange gods before me."

Discernment is a process of opening our hearts to God's truth. God alone can enlighten our hearts to understand the difference between truth and falsehood in every dimension of our lives and our culture.

Many today believe truth is relative, but in John's Gospel, Jesus tells Pilate that he was born and came into the world to testify to the truth. Jesus testifies to the truth about God, the truth about human nature and the truth about salvation. Pilate's infamous response is the hallmark of relativism: "What is truth?"

Despite all this, truth does exist, and the goal of discernment is to help us distinguish truth from falsehood in our own sacred story.

The original sin did not change God's love toward humanity. It simply redirected the divine love toward a massive rescue operation to save us from sin, darkness and death. Christ entrusted the church with a mission to highlight throughout all human history the truth about God, human nature and the salvation he won for us.

The spiritual exercise required of us daily is to open our hearts to God and to our sacred story. It will be God's grace and mercy that helps each of us unmask and slowly dismantle the profane story of self-centered love, just as St. Ignatius learned in his own life.

But you are not alone, for as you proceed on the Sacred Story prayer journey, you will discover that you are linked to the entire body of Christ in the church in this work of salvation. In your prayer and in your discernment, you will join Christ's great work of reconciliation for all of humanity and creation as you participate in the holy labor of returning body and soul to God.

The first goal of spiritual discernment is to identify truth vs. falsehood in your human nature, your identity as a child of God, and your relationship to God and His creation. The second goal of spiritual discernment is allowing God's grace to help you daily choose thoughts, words and deeds that express your authentic identity as a child of God.

St. Ignatius learned that there are three ways the human person can be "inspired." Inspirations can come from God, from the enemy of human nature and from ones' self. Next month's column will look in more depth at the three ways we can be inspired. Over the next four weeks, enter into your sacred story with the reflections and prayer exercises provided.

*Reflection—Your Two Narratives*

What thoughts, feelings or daydreams might reveal the *signature of God* in your *authentic* identity? What thoughts, feelings or daydreams might reveal the *signature of human nature's enemy* in your *false* identity? Pray for God's inspiration "to see and understand" both narratives in your history.

*Instructions for the Journey*

The school of discernment requires spiritual exercise. Most importantly, it requires listening, time, trial and error, prayer, patience and God's grace.

*Prayer Exercises*

Commit yourself to praying for 15 minutes daily (no more, no less) for the next four weeks —. Ponder how St. Ignatius' story links to your own life story. You also may pray the Sacred Story Examen Prayer found at sacredstory.net.

Part Four: Human Nature Willed by God

> "Although he was made by God in a state of holiness, from the very onset of his history man abused his liberty, at the urging of the Evil One. Man set himself against God and sought to attain his goal apart from God. Therefore man is split within himself. As a result, all of human life, whether individual or collective, shows itself to be a dramatic struggle between good and evil, between light and darkness" (Gaudium et Spes: *The Dignity of the Human Person* [13-15] ).

This excerpt from the Vatican II document summarizes well our previous reflections on the school of discernment.

God willed human nature as a perfect unity of body and spirit. Our body-spirit unity was possible because of our complete union of mind and heart with God. We were holy—we were "whole"—and thus immortal. In this state of original holiness—original justice—we did not need spiritual discernment.

Tragically, we chose independence from God. Our choice to be "masters of our own universe," shattered our interior unity of body and spirit. In this rupture, we confuse truth and falsehood, and easily lose touch with our authentic identity. At the age of thirty, Ignatius of Loyola awoke to the reality that he was living a profane story, not a sacred one. From that moment forward, St. Ignatius was tutored by God in the school of discernment to understand his authentic self—his sacred story—and to act accordingly in his thoughts, words and deeds.

To "enroll" in the school of discernment, we must understand our human nature as an enfleshed spirit. We must wake up to the spiritual world and the different elements that can shape us. Ignatius identified three elements: spiritual forces, spiritual inspirations and spiritual states or experiences.

*Spiritual Forces*

Two different spiritual forces vie to influence our human nature. One is the divine inspirer, whose inspirations lead to life and blessing. The other is the counter-inspirer, the one Ignatius called "the enemy of human nature," whose inspirations lead to death and curse.

*Spiritual Inspirations*

According to St. Ignatius, spiritual inspirations are capable of guiding our thoughts, words and deeds, and they originate from three distinct sources. Inspirations can originate from us, from the divine-inspirer or the enemy of human nature.

*Spiritual States*

St. Ignatius identified two spiritual states: consolation and desolation. Spiritual consolation is the feeling associated with an increase in faith, hope and love. Spiritual desolation is the feeling associated with a loss of faith, hope and love.

Discernment "wakes us up" to these spiritual forces, sources of inspiration, and spiritual states. We begin to see how they all influence our thoughts, words and deeds. For many of us, this awakening is gradual and progressive in nature, just as it was for St. Ignatius.

*Consolation and Desolation*

We will look at how the consolation and desolation work when originating from the Divine-inspirer and the counter-inspirer later. Let us consider how they work when they originate from our human nature in its blessing and brokenness.

When inspiration leading to consolation comes from us (i.e., from embedded strengths/gifts of our divinely crafted human nature), it could be a "bodily consolation" after an excellent workout that "life is good." It might also be an emotional experience of "happy to be alive", when beholding a baby or a beautiful sunset.

When inspiration leading to desolation comes from us (i.e., from embedded weakness/disease in our human nature broken by sin), it could result be a "bodily desolation" that "life is miserable" when we have a cold, flu or some type of injury. It might also be an emotional experience that "life is difficult, burdensome and not fair" when we are hurt in a relationship or suffer due to early-life events.

*The importance of Waking Up*

Why is it important to "wake up" to spiritual forces, inspirations and states? In a sermon, Bernard of Clairvaux said: "Once the eye of the soul has been purified by such considerations, we no longer abide within our spirit in a sense of sorrow, but abide rather in the Spirit of God with great delight."

It is vital that we become discerners, awakening to the spiritual forces, sources of inspirations, and the spiritual states of consolation or desolation. When we "wake up" we recognize how our unity with God, with ourselves, with others and with nature has been ruptured. With this recognition, we see that by God's grace, healing can begin in this life, be completed in the life to come. By waking up, we can live life as a sacred story.

Discernment is the essential starting point for cooperating fully with Christ's redeeming grace, won for us at great cost. Through discernment, we cooperate with God's massive rescue operation to save us from sin, darkness and death.

In the next article, we will expand our examination of consolation and desolation when originating from the Divine-inspirer and counter-inspirer, with two vital benchmark rules of discernment.

*Reflection*

You may continue your reflections on these spiritual realities by reading "On the Stages of Contemplation," a homily by St. Bernard of Clairvaux, and an expanded section of *Gaudium et Spes* (quoted at the start of this column). Find them at *www.NWCatholic.org*.

*Prayer Exercise*

Commit yourself over the next four weeks to praying daily for 15 minutes — no more, no less. Pray for the grace to discern the difference between inspirations in your life coming from the counter-inspirer, the enemy of human nature who passionately seeks your destruction, and those from the Divine-inspirer, the Creator who passionately loves you, and who desires your healing and joy.

Part Five: Consolation and Desolation

Learning about spiritual consolation and spiritual desolation benefit our sacred story journey. None of us will achieve perfection this side of eternity. Yet we know from Scripture and the teaching church that human nature was "perfect" once, and will be perfect again.

God *willed* human nature as a perfect unity of body and soul. The gift of human nature's perfection was lost in our original sin of turning toward self and away from God. God's world, created as a network of perfect relationship, suffered irreparable damage at every level: creature to Creator; body and soul, person to person, male and female and our relationship with creation. In this rupture our authentic identity was distorted. Our conscience was clouded and we lost sight of right and wrong. And most tragically, our hearts destined for perfect love and eternity, were broken by our sin that initiated violence, sickness and death.

But we were never abandoned. We have been helped all throughout salvation history and offered a path to return to God with all our hearts. Christ is our salvation. Our hope of regaining eternity is found in the grace and forgiveness of the Lord Jesus. Christ too always gives us saints to help us on our way. God used St. Ignatius' own brokenness to teach him spiritual discernment, which became his legacy to the body of Christ, to help us live our own sacred story.

Understanding Ignatius' discernment benchmarks as linked to spiritual consolation and spiritual desolation can help us immeasurably on our sacred story journey. In these benchmarks, we have guidelines to discern our desires for their authenticity so we can grow in faith, hope and love.

In the last selection we discussed three sources of "inspirations" in our lives: our own human nature (body and soul); the divine-inspirer; and human nature's enemy, the counter-inspirer. This week we consider two effects these inspirations have on us: spiritual consolation or spiritual desolation.

*First, a Vital Point…*

It is important to understand that divine inspiration, or consolation, does not always at first "feel good." Equally important is the realization that an unholy inspiration, or spiritual desolation, does not always at first "feel bad." We will explore this apparent paradox in a later column, but for now it is sufficient to recognize that both consolations and desolations influence the direction of our life either toward God or away from God in our thoughts, words and deeds.

*Consolation*

Consolation, the effect of authentic divine inspirations, can be discerned by its specific features. Consolations will always increase the heart's love for God and others. They will increase the virtues of docility, humility and self-generosity. Authentic consolations do not oppose the Scriptures, Tradition and the Teaching Church.

Consolations help you to choose thoughts, words and deeds that express your authentic human nature made in the divine image. They are the consequence of the divine physician's spirit working in you, helping to strengthen your heart and soul and encouraging you to turn your heart wholly to God.

*Desolation*

Counter-inspirations called desolations also have specific features. Desolations increase narcissism, displacing God and others. They will decrease docility and humility, and increase pride and self-satisfaction. Desolations may arouse hungers and desires that, although they can feel "right" or "okay", will typically contradict the truths and teachings proposed by Scripture, tradition and the teaching church.

Desolations are counter-inspirations because their author is opposed to Christ, and leads us away from life and truth. Counter-inspirations often produce desires that feel authentic because they are linked to fallen human nature's physical lusts and spiritual pride. They are the familiar default drives of a broken heart and a broken human nature. We must learn to identify these counter-inspirations — *discern* them — because they weaken our hearts and souls, encourage us to turn from God and choose thoughts, words and deeds that are opposed to our divinely-shaped human nature.

Ignatius' discernment wisdom becomes evident as we "wake up" and pay close attention to the effects of inspirations that lead to consolation and/or desolation in our daily lives. These spiritual movements act on us 24/7.

All of us are called to wake up and cooperate with God's grace for our healing and holiness. Christ encourages us to be not afraid, but to foster patience. The process of awakening to a life of spiritual discernment for our healing in Christ takes a lifetime.

*Reflection*

Awaken to life experiences that increase your love for God and others, increase the virtues of humility and generosity, and affirm the truths and teachings of Scripture, tradition and the teaching church. These life experiences could be a spiritual event of God's love, the beauty of nature, human love and forgiveness, a favorite Gospel passage.

Awaken to life experiences that displace God and others with an increase of pride and self-satisfaction, or arouse hungers and desires that contradict the truths and teachings of Scripture, tradition and the teaching church. These life experiences could be illnesses, injustice, addictions, broken relationships, angers.

*Prayer Exercise*

Repeat this affirmation aloud once or more a day for the next month:

*Christ, who has walked before me, shares my every burden.*

*Christ, who has walked before me, will help me resolve every crisis.*

*Christ, who has walked before me, knows my every hope.*

Part Six: You are an Eternal Prize to God and Satan

In our previous reflections, we've discussed how God (the divine-Inspirer), and the enemy of human nature (the counter inspirer), are both untiringly ambitious over how our story unfolds.

God seeks to influence our story for eternal love and life, while the enemy of human nature seeks to influence it for eternal despair and death. God desires eternal relationship for us, the enemy of human nature desires eternal loneliness.

If you have not yet established a 15-minute daily prayer time in a technology-free place, Lent is a particularly good time to do so. St. Ignatius suggested a regular daily prayer time as a means to deepen faith and wisdom and awaken to God's truth and love.

Beginning this Lent, make a commitment to pray for 15 minutes each day — no more and no less — and trust that with God's grace, this prayer will carry you through your entire life. As you pray, ask God for grace to discern the sources influencing your thoughts words and deeds, and whether it is God or the enemy of human nature shaping your daily inspirations. God will always answer our request for such insights.

*A Graced Awakening*

In past months we have discussed Ignatius' description of the three distinct sources that influence our thoughts, words, and deeds. These three are: our own interior life (emotional/intellectual); consolation (the divine inspiration drawing us in the direction of our authentic human nature); and desolation (the counter-inspiration of the enemy of our true human nature pulling us away from our authentic self).

Daily pay special attention to your emotions to discern these *spiritual states* of consolation and desolation. This process requires a graced awakening, so during your daily prayer times ask God for the "eyes to see" the characteristics and traits of consolation and desolation in your own story.

God desires to stir your conscience towards freedom and light, and bring you healing and hope. God knows your strengths and weaknesses. God will build on your strengths, kindle your holy desires and gradually heal what is wounded. The enemy of human nature also knows your strengths and weaknesses, and will seek to silence your conscience, magnify your problems, diminish your holy desires and gradually inspire hopelessness. Discernment is the habit of distinguishing between two different spiritual states by conscious awareness of their signature characteristics.

Spiritual Consolation — divine Inspiration — defines the feelings and thoughts of a healing heart returning to or residing in God. God always inspires movement towards reconciliation and union. Every increase in love, hope and faith that magnetizes your heart towards holy things, and all experiences of peace and quiet in the presence of your creator, are characteristics of consolation. The Divine inspiration of consolation is manifest in humility that views eternal life, lasting love, and faith in God as the hope of the single-hearted, and the ultimate goal of those "willing to risk seeing reality as it truly is."

Spiritual Desolation — counter-inspiration — is the direct opposite. Counter inspiration magnetizes a broken heart towards cynicism, lusts, isolation, anger, despair and loneliness. The counter inspiration of desolation is manifest in an unyielding pride that views eternal life, lasting love, and faith in God as illusions of the simple-minded.

If you are accustomed to physical pleasures or lifestyles and relationships that fall outside the boundaries of the Commandments or church teaching, the inspiration to cut loose from those pleasures can make you feel distress and anxiety. During his own awakening, St. Ignatius panicked and felt distress when he realized that he would have to live without such pleasures for the rest of his life.

Counter inspirations can make you "feel good" even if they move you away from your authentic human nature. The counter-inspiration may encourage feelings of complacency, to "just stay where you are." The fears aroused by the invitation to live authentically need to be strongly confronted because the counter-inspirations are inviting you toward death, not life.

*Pray for the Grace of Discernment*

Both consolation and desolation can "feel" good or bad, depending on your lifestyle and the corresponding state of your heart and soul. To assist your discernment, pay attention to the definitions of authenticity regarding human nature as defined by the Commandments and church teaching. And remember to pray for the grace to "wake up."

*Reflection*

Think about the things that make you feel good and the things that make you feel bad. Consider whether these things are moving you toward union with God and reconciliation or undermining your faith in God and leading to cynicism and isolation.

*Prayer Exercise*

Commit yourself to praying for 15 minutes daily (no more, no less) over the next four weeks . Pray for the grace to discern the difference between inspirations in your life that come from God and those counter-inspirations that come from human nature's enemy.


Part Seven: Are You Moving Toward Life or Death?

Your preferred lifestyles and sub-cultures can tell you about the direction of your story. One of the practices that can help shape your life as sacred story is celebrating sacramental reconciliation monthly. A helpful preparation for reconciliation — or confession as it is commonly known — is an examination of the embedded attitudes or lifestyles that shape your life story. These attitudes, lifestyles, and sub-cultures are far more significant than we may think!

As we've learned in previous columns, we consciously or unconsciously align our stories toward or away from God—toward life or death. The book of Deuteronomy captures this reality as God places two distinct choices before the people of Israel: "Here, then, I have today set before you life and prosperity, death and doom." (Dt. 30:15)

This Scripture passage can serve as a guideline for examining our consciences. It's an invitation to discern the good in our life from the evil. The spiritual inspirations of consolation and desolation mark the points where our path is set toward God and life as a sacred story, or departing from that path toward "death and doom."

One method for approaching this process of discernment — this examination of conscience — is to consider what kind of cultures or sub-cultures we inhabit on a daily basis and what these tell us about whether we are moving toward or away from the author of life.

*Listen to Your Heart*

The commandments, Scripture and the teaching church propose a life that moves us toward a sacred story that will bear eternal fruit. On the other hand, when we choose to align ourselves with sub-cultures that are counter to the commandments, Scripture and church, it becomes more difficult to recognize anti-Gospel lifestyles that move us toward death and curse.

These anti-Gospel sub-cultures can be economic, political, artistic, ethnic, intellectual, sexual, athletic, addiction-based and technology-based, just to name a few. Even if a sub-culture is not inherently anti-Gospel, the primary danger is that we can easily "cocoon" ourselves in these cultures, allowing their definitions of happiness, success, the good, the beautiful and the moral to *isolate* us from the data coming from deep in our heart, or from any other source.

The data we want to pay attention to are those inspirations we have been considering in previous installment. It is most important to keep an eye on the *direction* the inspirations lead you, more than whether individual inspirations make you feel good or feel bad. This may seem counter-intuitive – how could an inspiration that "feels" bad actually be a sign that we are on the right path?

This can occur because Divine inspiration (spiritual consolation) is a healthy lifestyle that may not "feel" healthy because it is not supported by the culture surrounding you. Counter inspiration (spiritual desolation), on the other hand, is an unhealthy lifestyle that might not feel unhealthy because it is supported by the culture or sub-cultures in which you live. It is just like physical health – even though we know it is unhealthy, it still "feels" good to sit around eating junk food if that is our accustomed habit and environment!

*Identify Signature Characteristics*

It is often helpful to map some of the influences in your life. Make a small chart of the various sub-cultures where you spend most of your time: corporate culture, work environments, websites, social groups and associations, exercise or athletic environments, groups aligned with arts or entertainment, political parties and the cultures of film, television or radio.

Next to each sub-culture, write what you believe is its signature characteristic regarding its overall influence on your lifestyle. Does the sub-culture support divine inspiration or support counter inspiration? In other words, is the sub-culture congruent with the values of the commandments, Scripture and the teaching and tradition of the church?

Do you have what St. Ignatius would call an "inordinate attachment" to any of these sub-cultures and the values they espouse? Does your affiliation with the sub-culture move you further along in your sacred story or does it obstruct your movement?

You can identify the trajectory of your story — and better prepare yourself for the sacrament of Reconciliation — by reflecting on how you live and whether your lifestyle is influenced by the divine-inspirer or the counter-inspirer. One way of just staying alert to your story is to take stock of whether the balance of thoughts, words and deeds are in tune with the commandments, Scripture and the teaching church.

If not, then you can examen your story and ask God for insight as to what can lead you to living more in tune with life as Sacred Story.

*How to Discern Inspirations*

*Divine Inspirations*

If your thoughts, words and deeds are aligned with Scripture, commandments and the teaching church, the divine author of your human nature will awaken your reason, stir your conscience and provide "heart-verification" of thoughts, words and deeds that can move you off the true path.

God grants feelings of sadness, concern, grief and remorse when you are moving towards the counter inspirations of anti-love — anti-Christ. Such feelings can be difficult and intense. Yet they are a gift and a certain reminder that engaging the Gospel values of your faith will bring you the peace and hope you seek.

*Counter Inspirations*

If your thoughts, words and deeds are opposed to the commandments, Scripture and the teaching church, the enemy of human nature is able to hold you in the grip of your disordered appetites by deceit and false appearances. What leads you away from God, from love, may appear pleasurable, good, life-giving, fashionable, enlightened and sophisticated.

These false loves speak powerfully to broken hearts. If you are in the grip of counter inspirations you may feel aversion to engaging Gospel values or be hostile to the commandments and guidelines of the teaching church. You may experience difficulty practicing and persevering in your faith.

Part Eight: Why Does God Allow Spiritual Desolation?

St. Ignatius himself experienced the loss of faith, hope and love. From this he offers insights for dealing with spiritual darkness. Whether we are aware of it or not, each of us is influenced by spiritual inspirations throughout our lives. We are always either in a state of consolation or desolation. We may be oblivious to these spiritual states unless we enter a "school of discernment" and learn how to become aware of their influence.

In the last reflection we explored definitions of spiritual consolation and spiritual desolation as embedded attitudes or lifestyles that can shape our life story. This month we will consider St. Ignatius' wisdom on the reasons for spiritual desolation and his advice for our response.

As we considered in previous columns, when we experience a loss of faith, hope, and love when we are in the grip of desolation. Why would God allow this?

*Three Reasons for Spiritual Desolation*

St. Ignatius discerned that desolation is the result of following the false logic of counter inspirations. When we make wrong choices in our thoughts, words and deeds, God allows us to experience the darkness of our sins as a holy warning. This experience of desolation is meant to stir our consciences and return us to authenticity.

The second reason God allows desolation is directly linked with our human growth and spiritual progress. God wants to awaken our whole being — spirit, mind and body — to become aware of our hidden wounds.

Desolation reveals the ways in which sin has taken root in our spirits, minds and bodies. Spiritual progress is possible only when we "wake up" and confront these damaging patterns.

We might feel discouraged by the darkness in our hearts, minds and bodies at such times. In this moment however, we must re-affirm our hope in the Lord, who is gradually uprooting the source of the darkness in our being, with our cooperation. Ignatius reminds us that when we feel lost, God is closer to us than ever.

Third, desolation may appear during times of spiritual advancement. One example might be a period of peace in divine inspiration after a period of purification marked by struggle. At such times, we may be tempted to believe that we have "arrived," and have reached the end of our spiritual journey.

This is an illusion. When we find ourselves in these moments of pride and self-satisfaction, , the counter inspirations of desolation return. God allows desolations at these times as a warning, to remind us that although we have grown in authenticity and holiness, we are still susceptible to the narcissism and destructive pride that will halt all our progress.

In addition to identifying the reasons God allows desolation, Ignatius developed guidelines for how we should act when we feel the discouragement, hopelessness and frustration that accompany it.

*Four Guidelines*

First, St. Ignatius taught that we should never change course when in desolation. Ignatius warns that it is a clear sign of counter inspirations at work when we feel compelled by an "anxious urgency" to reach a decision or engage an action.

Second, during times of desolation we need to redouble our efforts to open and orient our hearts to God, even if it feels useless. Prayer, examination of conscience and simple penance or fasting is helpful as we seek God's grace. (Mk 9:29)

The third guideline is to remember that God will give us the grace we need, building on our natural abilities. When we feel overwhelmed by temptations, or the darkness of spirit associated with disordered attractions and compulsive behaviors, there is always sufficient grace for salvation, even if the counter inspiration indicates otherwise.

Finally, we must be intentional in our efforts to cultivate patience and perseverance in the religious practices of our faith when influenced by the counter inspiration of desolation. "Nothing in the past or the future; no angel or demon; no height or depth; nothing in all of creation will ever separate you from my love in Christ Jesus." (Rom 8:38-39)

Remember that God holds you fast during the divine inspirations of consolation, and holds you even closer during the cleansing times of desolation. Affirm your faith in God. Hold fast to your spiritual disciplines and the practices of your faith. Seek stability and fidelity both in times of peace and calm and in times of turbulence and struggle.

Next time, we'll consider some of the strategies the enemy employs to attack our authentic human nature and obstruct our spiritual progress.

Want to learn more?

Visit www.sacredstory.net and purchase "Forty Weeks: An Ignatian Path to Christ with Sacred Story Prayer"

Part Nine: Why Bother with Spiritual Discernment?

Discovering how our hearts have been broken allows the divine physician to heal us so we can produce fruit that endures to eternity. Some who have followed past columns in this series may wonder about the practical importance of spiritual discernment in our daily lives. Does the spiritual battle between the divine inspirer and the enemy of human nature make any difference in how I live my life?

A story reported in the news media might help. A teenager won a court case, forcing a public high school to remove a banner in the school's gym that referred to "Our Heavenly Father." The student, a baptized Roman Catholic, stopped believing in God at ten years of age when their mother fell ill.

*A wounded, Broken Heart*

"I had always been told that if you pray, God will always be there when you need Him," the student said. "And it didn't happen for me, and I doubted it had happened for anybody else. So yeah, I think that was just like the last step, and after that I just really didn't believe any of it."

Much of the media framed the story as a legal and constitutional fight to prevent state-sponsored religion. But another plotline can be detected in this story. The student is opposing religious expression because of deep childhood wounds.

At the bottom of this story is a deeply wounded heart. The student's mother fell ill and "God did not listen" to a prayer for healing. If we look only on the surface, we see a determined and fearless youth standing up against the wrath of classmates and townspeople to defend constitutional rights.

This student may be at the beginning of a life-long crusade, and the enemy of human nature will urge them on in this fight. The enemy will keep this person distracted from the interior wound so it cannot be healed. And so it is with all of us.

Unless we "wake up" to our spiritual nature, we are blind to our emotional and intellectual defense systems. The defenses of pride and their adult intellectual justifications conceal the fear and pain of a 10-year-old child's broken heart.

*Three Lines of Attack*

The enemy of human nature uses three principal attack strategies to obstruct our spiritual progress. All three use elements of our life story as weapons against us: our unconscious fears, our psychological and spiritual vulnerabilities and our long-standing addictions.

Ignatius learned the three attack strategies during his own conversion process. These strategies are designed to confound, discourage and deceive individuals committed to spiritual growth. The primary weapon in all three strategies is *fear*.

The first strategy is direct fear and "panic attacks." If you stay committed to the process of uprooting vices, sins, addictions and destructive habits from your life and heart, you may suffer waves of fear and panic. These are meant to turn you away from the healing process.

Those committed to growing in holiness will also confront a second strategy: Narcissism and false values masquerading as true love and authentic values. The enemy can portray our narcissism as authentic love and vices as positive values, but these false loves are only mirages for our parched and anxious hearts. Instead of providing lasting peace, these illusions merely intensify our longings, self-deception, and self-preoccupation.

The third line of attack is directed at the spiritual and psychological wounds that make you most vulnerable. The enemy's purpose is to keep your emotional and intellectual defenses firmly in place, hardening your judgments. This keeps your conscience dark and your true human nature hidden. This third strategy is perhaps the most insidious. This is the way the enemy manipulated the young "atheist", and it is often the way the enemy of human nature manipulates us as well.

*Fruit that Endures to Eternity*

Like the teenage crusader, many people fighting apparently noble causes might only be terrified, wounded children running away from their pain. One thinks of St. Paul's attacks on the church before his conversion. At the opening of the Acts of the Apostles, Saul witnessed the murder of Stephen, and went on to crusade against all followers of the Way. (Acts 9:1-2)

The enemy of human nature manipulated Saul's anger, cloaking his homicidal rage in religious justifications. Fear was likely at the root of Saul's rage. It is possible that fear was also a driving force in St. Ignatius' life when, against the advice of others, he engaged in a futile battle that nearly ended his life.

Much of the violence perpetrated between persons, groups and countries in our own day is generated by wounded hearts seeking revenge for their suffering (consciously or otherwise).

In your own discernment, observe how the enemy of human nature instigates intellectual arguments, fosters a sense of injustice, and promotes defiance against legitimate authority. Ask the Lord, "What motivates my crusade (or crusades)? Where do I hurt?" Ask the Lord to help you heal, receive forgiveness and to forgive others so that you may spend the energy of your life producing fruit that endures to eternity.

*Part Ten: Develop your Spiritual Radar*

St. Ignatius learned he couldn't save himself and discovered radical, loving trust in God. We began this series of short reflections on discernment by acknowledging that we are heirs to the broken relationships that resulted from original sin. We also acknowledged our faith that God's work in creation could not and would not be undone by sin.

These articles have been a brief introduction to a "school of discernment" in the tradition established by St. Ignatius of Loyola. The lessons are designed to let God heal our human nature, by restoring our original unity of body and spirit in keeping with the Divine plan.

Over the past weeks, we learned that Ignatius' discernment insights resulted from a crippling battle with scruples. When he turned away from his former self-centered and self-assertive way of life to follow Jesus, he was given the grace to see that the pride and narcissism that nearly led to his death were still at work in him under the "holy" guise of obsessively re-confessing his past sins.

*Subtle Deceptions*

As far as Ignatius was concerned, if he could not save himself, and do it his way, he would not do it at all. This was his narcissistic pride, plain and simple. The enemy of human nature had turned Ignatius' good habit against him.

Ignatius was still trying to be master of his own universe. In trying to save himself, he was being tempted to remove God from the equation. Eventually he was given grace to observe that this subtle deception of fixating on his sinfulness was taking him away from God, and the new life of living as a disciple of Jesus.

Since the fall of our first parents — original sin — all of us have difficulty differentiating between divine inspirations and counter-inspirations. By grace, Ignatius discovered the difference, and his guidelines for discernment have brought countless thousands to Christ, helping them to live life as a sacred story.

Ignatius still teaches us to examine the trajectory of our thoughts and desires. If our thoughts lead us in a direction contrary to the Ten Commandments and the precepts of Christ, or they weaken our aspirations for selflessness and diminish our good plans and goals, then they are counter inspirations.

When Ignatius recognized that his own aspirations for conversion were undermined by his obsessive re-confession of past sins, he surrendered the damaging habit. This choice, and the discovery of his spiritual radar, initiated the saint's process for dismantling his narcissistic pride at its root. It also initiated a new era of spiritual discernment for the church.

*A Docility and Willingness to Surrender*

When we enter St. Ignatius' school of discernment, we awaken to the depth of our emotions, and we begin to identify their trajectory so we can interpret them accurately. In other words, we begin using our God-given spiritual radar.

Inspirations of the divine-inspirer reliably produce an intense sense of devotion and love of God and of innocence. They produce a sense of selflessness and willing surrender of our life to God's control. These inspirations have an openness of spirit as their trademark, encouraging us to hear and trust received tradition, the commandments, and the precepts of Christ as proclaimed by the church.

Counter inspirations, on the other hand, have an arrogant pride as their trademark, encouraging us to distrust received tradition, the commandments, and the precepts of Christ as proclaimed by the church. These counter-inspirations work toward disintegration and a weakening of our holy commitments and resolutions.

Ignatius once remarked that human beings are no match for the subtle temptations of the enemy of human nature. But God is! The saint advises us to trust our life, our heart and our soul to Christ, who will deal with the enemy for us.

The divine-inspirer will always offer us the graces and insights to lead us home. God's victory is assured for us in Christ's birth, life, death and resurrection. Our sure hope is in him and he will help us just as he helped St. Ignatius.

And remember. You should not be discouraged by your failings, your sins and weaknesses. The divine physician never tires of forgiving you and you should never tire of going to him for forgiveness. In this radical, loving relationship, you will always encounter the unfathomable and unbounded mercy of God who seeks to transform your life into a sacred story.

# Chapter Four

## THE TEN COMMANDMENTS
## GOD'S RELATIONAL CODES

When we look at creation, the fall and redemption from the perspective of relationships, we can discern new significance in the "revealed" moral codes we call the Decalogue or the Ten Commandments. Let's briefly review where we have come from before looking anew at the Ten Commandments.[35]

God is a relationship of three distinct persons who are *completely* one because God is Love! God is a relationship of love. God creates a relational universe with persons made in God's image and likeness. The purpose for this utterly gratuitous act of creation is to freely share love with beings who can share in God's love. Love is creative, love is generous and love is self-less.

For persons made in God's image and likeness, it was necessary that their "human nature" be comprised of both body and spirit. This relationship of body and spirit enabled beings to communicate with God who, prior to Christ, is entirely spiritual. And the full communication—the full and complete *communion*—of persons with God so energized the "body and soul" that human nature was gifted with immortality. This was

---

[35] "What good deed must I do, to have eternal life?" - "If you would enter into life, keep the commandments" (*Mt* 19:16-17). By his life and by his preaching Jesus attested to the permanent validity of the Decalogue. The gift of the Decalogue is bestowed from within the covenant concluded by God with his people. God's commandments take on their true meaning in and through this covenant. In fidelity to Scripture and in conformity with Jesus' example, the tradition of the Church has always acknowledged the primordial importance and significance of the Decalogue. The Decalogue forms an organic unity in which each "word" or "commandment" refers to all the others taken together. To transgress one commandment is to infringe the whole Law (cf. *Jas* 2:10-11). The Decalogue contains a privileged expression of the natural law. It is made known to us by divine revelation and by human reason. The Ten Commandments, in their fundamental content, state grave obligations. However, obedience to these precepts also implies obligations in matter which is, in itself, light. What God commands he makes possible by his grace. CCC: 2075-2082.

God's plan: that God who is the *essence* of Life and Love would share with those created in God's image and likeness this gift of love and life for eternity. The condition for this immortal gift was to remain in full communion with God.

God created the cosmos and God created human nature. It cannot be undone or changed without consequences. As longs as full communion is maintained, *unity in diversity* is possible. This unity in diversity is a participation in the very experience of the Trinity who is a complete unity in a diversity of persons—three persons in one God. God gifted human nature to share in a manner appropriate to our creature-hood, being a unique person but fully sharing in the joy of relationship with God and others. To be fully open to giving and receiving love while simultaneously maintaining one's unique identity is the ultimate desire of the human heart. No wonder: because we are *made* in "the image and likeness of God."

The tragedy of the original temptation and the Original Sin comes fully into view. This was a grand deception: that persons made in God's image could maintain their immortality, their individuality and the joy of love and communion by turning from God to self. C. S. Lewis had a unique rendition of this turning to self in his novel *Perelandra*.[36] In turning to self away from God, the sacred diversity would collapse into an unholy diversity. In this new unholy diversity, individual personalities will assert their own power and seek to define human nature apart from God.

When we "creatures" broke our full communion with God—our full relationship—we lost both our unique identities and the possibility for relationships without strife or struggle. We lost sacred diversity and opened the world to its unholy opposite: self-centered individuality that will seek to assert its independence from God. We also lost our immortality. There are only two persons "born in time" who were both free from sin and its effects; the Blessed Mother and her son, Jesus. The Blessed Mother we affirm was preserved from the corruption of death.[37] Christ of course, was preserved from all corruption and is the first fruits of creation:

> *"You who are Israelites, hear these words. Jesus the Nazorean was a man commended to you by God with mighty deeds, wonders, and signs, which God worked through him in your midst, as you yourselves know. This man, delivered up by the set plan and foreknowledge of God, you killed, using lawless men to crucify him. But God raised him up, releasing him from the throes of death, because it was impossible for him to be held by it. For David says of him: 'I saw the*

---

[36] We call this thing a mirror. A man can love himself, and be together with himself. That is what it means to be a man or a woman--to walk alongside oneself as if one were a second person and to delight in one's own beauty. Mirrors are made to teach us this art. Lewis, C. S. *Perelandra*. 1944. New York: Macmillan, 1965. (137).

[37] "Finally the Immaculate Virgin, preserved free from all stain of original sin, when the course of her earthly life was finished, was taken up body and soul into heavenly glory, and exalted by the Lord as Queen over all things, so that she might be the more fully conformed to her Son, the Lord of lords and conqueror of sin and death."[508] The Assumption of the Blessed Virgin is a singular participation in her Son's Resurrection and an anticipation of the resurrection of other Christians: In giving birth you kept your virginity; in your Dormition you did not leave the world, O Mother of God, but were joined to the source of Life. You conceived the living God and, by your prayers, will deliver our souls from death. CCC: 966.

*Lord ever before me, with him at my right hand I shall not be disturbed. Therefore my heart has been glad and my tongue has exulted; my flesh, too, will dwell in hope, because you will not abandon my soul to the netherworld, nor will you suffer your holy one to see corruption."*
Acts 2: 22-27.

But at the time of our fall from obedience to the voice of God, God planned a way to restore everything. God prepares a people, Israel, to become the vehicle for bringing humanity back into communion union with God by teaching the world what constitutes right relationships. At Christ's birth "in the fullness of time" God now inaugurates the Church that will be the vehicle for restoring the unity of all people in Christ.

The first creation is God's gift to us. And God begins the work of restoring creation after the fall with the people of Israel, the Decalogue and the Covenant at Sinai. And God completes the work of re-creation with the New Covenant in Christ and the Church. Just as Christ is the principle of salvation for everyone:

*He is 'the stone rejected by you, the builders, which has become the cornerstone.' There is no salvation through anyone else, nor is there any other name under heaven given to the human race by which we are to be saved."* Acts 4: 11-12.

So the Church will be the chosen community for this universal work of redemption in Christ.

*To reunite all his children, scattered and led astray by sin, the Father willed to call the whole of humanity together into his Son's Church. The Church is the place where humanity must rediscover its unity and salvation. The Church is "the world reconciled." She is that bark which "in the full sail of the Lord's cross, by the breath of the Holy Spirit, navigates safely in this world." According to another image dear to the Church Fathers, she is prefigured by Noah's ark, which alone saves from the flood. "Outside the Church there is no salvation:" How are we to understand this affirmation, often repeated by the Church Fathers? Re-formulated positively, it means that all salvation comes from Christ the Head through the Church which is his Body: Basing itself on Scripture and Tradition, the Council teaches that the Church, a pilgrim now on earth, is necessary for salvation: the one Christ is the mediator and the way of salvation; he is present to us in his body which is the Church. He himself explicitly asserted the necessity of faith and Baptism, and thereby affirmed at the same time the necessity of the Church which men enter through Baptism as through a door. Hence they could not be saved who, knowing that the Catholic Church was founded as necessary by God through Christ, would refuse either to enter it or to remain in it. This affirmation is not aimed at those who, through no fault of their own, do not know Christ and his Church: Those who, through no fault of their own, do not know the Gospel of Christ or his Church, but who nevertheless seek God with a sincere heart, and, moved by grace, try in their actions to do his will as they know it through the dictates of their conscience - those too may achieve eternal salvation. "Although in ways known to himself God can lead those who, through no fault of their own, are ignorant of the Gospel, to that faith without which it is impossible to please him, the Church still has the obligation and also the sacred right to evangelize all men."*[38]

The beginning of the new creation with the people of Israel is Christ and the Church are God's gifts to us. And the revealed truths of the faith are also God's gift to us to guide us on our way back home. It is in this light that we can view the Ten Commandments God's to all humanity to helps us remember what constitutes right relationships. We teach them to our children not as rules that we must obey us but as lifelines to help us constantly remember what constitute "right relationships." They help us know how we can create the right relationships to reconnect with God and others in our own Sacred Story. Indeed, as the Psalmist says, those who follow God's laws will be blessed!

> *Though princes meet and talk against me,*
> *Your servant meditates on your statutes.*
> *Yes, your decrees are my delight;*
> *They are my counselors.*
> *I declared my ways, and you answered me;*
> *Teach me your statutes.*
> *Make me understand the way of your precepts,*
> *And I will meditate on your wondrous deeds.*
> *Remove from me the way of falsehood,*
> *And favor me with your law.*
> *The way of truth I have chosen;*
> *I have set your ordinances before me.*
> *Blessed are they who follow the law of the Lord!*
> Ps 119: 23-24, 26-27, 29-30.

Therefore, the Decalogue or the Commandments are a blessing to humanity. Many have made the case that the success of Western civilization is due in large measure to the influence of Judeo-Christian values in legal systems, social systems, educational systems and medicine. The efforts on the part of some municipalities to enshrine the Ten Commandments by making of them a public display oftentimes is motivated by the significant civilizing force for the human social good that has issued forth from these basic *relational codes*. They are Commandments that can help all of humanity understand what leads to hope, peace and social balance. They are no longer just for "believers." Here is how the Catechism of the Catholic Church contextualizes the Ten Commandments as "revealed truths" in light of God, Creation, the fall and God's

---
[38] CCC 845-848.

promise to restore relationship with humanity who broke relationship with God. Why, because God loved us first![39]

> The "ten words" are pronounced by God in the midst of a theophany ("The LORD spoke with you face to face at the mountain, out of the midst of the fire." Dt 5:4). They belong to God's revelation of himself and his glory. The gift of the Commandments is the gift of God himself and his holy will. In making his will known, God reveals himself to his people. The gift of the commandments and of the Law is part of the covenant God sealed with his own. In *Exodus*, the revelation of the "ten words" is granted between the proposal of the covenant and its conclusion - after the people had committed themselves to "do" all that the Lord had said, and to "obey" it. The Decalogue is never handed on without first recalling the covenant ("The LORD our God made a covenant with us in Horeb.").
>
> The Commandments take on their full meaning within the covenant. According to Scripture, man's moral life has all its meaning in and through the covenant. The first of the "ten words" recalls that God loved his people first:
>
> *Since there was a passing from the paradise of freedom to the slavery of this world, in punishment for sin, the first phrase of the Decalogue, the first word of God's commandments, bears on freedom "I am the LORD your God, who brought you out of the land of Egypt, out of the house of slavery."*[40]
>
> The Commandments properly so-called come in the second place: they express the implications of belonging to God through the establishment of the covenant. Moral existence is a *response* to the Lord's loving initiative. It is the acknowledgement and homage given to God and a worship of thanksgiving. It is cooperation with the plan God pursues in history.
>
> The covenant and dialogue between God and man are also attested to by the fact that all the obligations are stated in the first person ("I am the Lord.") and addressed by God to another personal subject ("you"). In all God's commandments, the singular personal pronoun designates the recipient. God makes his will known to each person in particular, at the same time as he makes it known to the whole people:
>
> *The Lord prescribed love towards God and taught justice towards neighbor, so that man would be neither unjust, nor unworthy of God. Thus, through the Decalogue, God prepared man to*

---

[39] This selected text is from, CCC, #'s 2059-2063.

[40] Origen, *Hom. in Ex.* 8,1:PG 12,350; cf. Ex 20:2; Deut 5:6.

*become his friend and to live in harmony with his neighbor. . . . The words of the Decalogue remain likewise for us Christians. Far from being abolished, they have received amplification and development from the fact of the coming of the Lord in the flesh.*[41]

How are the Commandments structured? The first Three Commandments reveal God as our primary relationship because God is the origin and giver of all life. The command to love the Lord with all our mind, heart and strength is the only way we can have life because we are made in God's image and likeness. God made us to be in communion with God and it is the only path to life, happiness and peace.

The last Seven Commandments affirm that being made in God's image and likeness, we are to love everyone God made as we would love and reverence our very self. By loving our neighbor as ourselves, we participate in God's loving plan for all of creation. Not to love our neighbor as ourselves, is to break relationship with God because I break relationship with those made in God's image and likeness.

The Commandments as revealed truths that summarize the codes for restoring humankind's relationship with God and toward one's neighbor are a cohesive unit even though they are ten in number:

> The Decalogue forms a coherent whole. Each "word" refers to each of the others and to all of them; they reciprocally condition one another. The two tables shed light on one another; they form an organic unity. To transgress one commandment is to infringe all the others.[30] One cannot honor another person without blessing God his Creator. One cannot adore God without loving all men, his creatures. The Decalogue brings man's religious and social life into unity.[42]

*The Commandments as Relational Codes*

### THE FIRST RELATIONAL CODE

*I am the Lord your God, you shall have no strange gods before me.*

---

[41] St. Irenaeus, *Adv. haeres.*, 4,16, 3-4:PG 7/1,1017-1018.
[42] CCC # 2069.

I believe God loved me into life and I commit to this relationship by giving all my mind, heart and strength to God alone and promise daily that I will serve no other god:

As a child created by God I can only have life and love if I keep Him at the center of my heart. I will daily remember to try and put God first in everything I say, think and do. If I forget that I am completely dependent on God, I will make idols of created goods. These idols can only enslave me. I will be enslaved if I worship my accomplishments, my things or famous people.

*Action:* Each morning as I wake up I can say, "Good morning, God. This is _____, the child you love and created!"

## THE SECOND RELATIONAL CODE

*You shall not take the name of the Lord your God in vain*

I believe God loved me into life and I commit myself to the relationship by always adoring and reverencing the name of God!

As a child of God I have been privileged to know God's name. A name is sacred because it defines the person's identity. To disrespect the name is to destroys my reverence for the person and undermines the foundation for my relationship with them.

*Action:* I am called to protect my relationship with God by honoring all of the names for God. I hurt myself if I use God's name in anger, frustration or use it casually without reverence.

## THE THIRD RELATIONAL CODE

*Remember to keep holy the Sabbath day.*

I believe God loved me into life and I commit myself to the relationship by always dedicating the Sabbath Day as one of praising, reverencing and serving God. As God's child I am called to keep my relationship with Him at the center of my life by dedicating the Sabbath as God's day. The Sabbath creates a space for me to focus on the most important relationship for my life and happiness. If I organize my life so that being with God is not the center of the Sabbath, I violate the First Commandment harm my changes of allowing this relationship to grow.

*Action:* I remember to be thankful on this day and to rest in God's love for me and all other people. I make the Sabbath special by always attending Mass, singing and praying the Mass prayers. I will be especially attentive on the Sabbath because I know that God wants to communicate with me in the Holy Eucharist. I can be open to God too by being attentive to my family and other parishioners. I will be a minister at Mass when I am able.

## THE FOURTH RELATIONAL CODE

*Honor your Father and Mother*

I believe God loved me into life and so I commit myself to the relationship with my parents who through God's power gave me life. As a child of God I am called to honor the relationship with my parents. They have participated in God's creative love by saying "yes" to your being born. When you love them, you can also love God more. As we grow older, we have the opportunity to imitate God's love by caring for them and forgiving them of any shortcomings or failings.

*Action:* I will listen to my parents and appreciate their efforts to feed, clothe, house and educate me. I will thank them. I will respect my parents because they love and care for me. I will speak of them with respect as this shows my love for God.

## THE FIFTH RELATIONAL CODE

*You Shall Not Kill*

I believe God loved me into life and so I commit myself to a relationship with all those made in God's image and likeness by vowing to do nothing to hurt anyone. As a child of God I am called to love my neighbor who like me, is made in God's image. To violate them in any way (from cultivating hate to physical harm) is a grave offense that also violates my relationship with God.

*Action:* I will respect all people in what I say, think and do. I will be kind and not to others in my speech, through bully behaviors or by fighting. I will reverence the life God gave to me by my lifestyle and habits and by what I do to my body. I will build relationships on respect for others.

## THE SIXTH AND NINTH RELATIONAL CODES

*You shall not commit adultery &*
*You shall not covet your neighbor's spouse*

I believe God loved me into life and so I commit myself never to break relationship with my spouse or work to have another break theirs either. As a child of God I am called to keep my relationship with God at the center of my life by respecting the relationship between husband and wife which is a sacred bond that mirrors the unity and fruitful love of the Trinity. To misuse any element of the romantic or sexual nature of persons divides me against my very self, which is meat for self-gift.

*Action:* I will respect my own and others' bodies by developing modest habits and not tempting others to indecent behaviors. In honoring all relationships I see God in others and treat them as I would treat God. I will ask God to help me not act on unholy desires that would harm relationships and break hearts.

## THE SEVENTH AND TENTH RELATIONAL CODES

*You shall not steal and &*
*You shall not covet your neighbor's goods*

I believe God loved me into life and so I commit myself never to break relationship with anyone by taking from them what does not belong to me or even desire to do so! As a child of God I am called to keep God at the center of my life by always respecting what belongs to others. The proper use of creation is a basic element of our relationship with other human persons, and basic to honoring the Creator of all that is.

*Action:* I will have a goal not to use more than I need or to be attached to "things" (whether present or future). I will strive to find God in all things, and never focus things as valuable ends in themselves. Things are valuable only if they can lead me to God.

*Action:* I keep my relationship with God by being honest about what belongs to others and giving thanks for what God has given to me to use. I will cultivate a spirit of thanksgiving even for what God has given to others and pray they use these gifts in service of God and others. This will help me not to desire what others have and make me more grateful for what I have been given. In all of this, I will ask God to help me realize that my relationship with Him and my brothers and sisters is always more important than things I can possesses.

## THE EIGHTH RELATIONAL CODE

*You shall not bear false witness against your neighbor.*

I believe God loved me into life and so I commit myself never to break relationship with anyone by my false or destructive words or speech! As a child of God I am called to keep my relationship with God at the center of my life. I do this by my respectful speech toward my brothers and sisters. Saying mean or hateful things about my brothers and sisters, even when they might be true, breaks my relationship with them and with God, because God is love.

*Action:* I will do this by not saying things that even if true, can hurt the heart and the reputation of a brother or a sister. I will not lie about others to make myself look better in other's eyes. I will always find something positive to say about a person that others are laughing at or disrespecting, even when I might be rejected by them. I will pray not to be jealous of others' friendships or attempt to hurt them if I am jealous. I will strive to treat others the way I want to be treated by them. This way, I keep my relationship with God.

# ABOUT THE AUTHOR

Fr. William Watson, S.J., D. Min., has spent over thirty years developing Ignatian programs and retreats. Fr. Watson has served as: Director of Retreat Programs at Georgetown University; Vice President for Mission at Gonzaga University; and Provincial Assistant for International Ministries for the Oregon Province of the Society of Jesus. He holds Masters Degrees in Divinity and Pastoral Studies, respectively (1986; Weston Jesuit School of Theology, Cambridge Massachusetts). He received his Doctor of Ministry degree in 2009 from The Catholic University of America (Washington D.C.).

In the spring of 2011 Fr. Watson launched the non-profit Sacred Story Institute, to bring Ignatian Spirituality to Catholics of all ages and walks of life. The Sacred Story Institute is promoting third millennium evangelization for the Society of Jesus and the Church by using the time-tested *Examination of Conscience* of St. Ignatius.

# Sacred Story Press
# Seattle, Washington, USA
## sacredstorypress.com

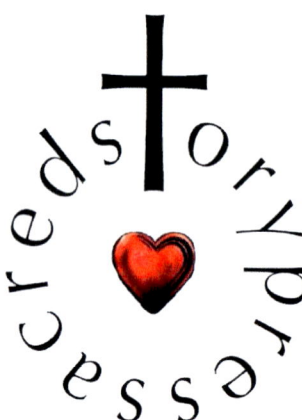

Sacred Story Press explores dynamic new dimensions of classic Ignatian spirituality, based on St. Ignatius' Conscience Examen in the *Sacred Story* prayer method pioneered by Fr. Bill Watson, S.J. We are creating a new class of spiritual resources. Our publications are research-based, authentic to the Catholic Tradition and designed to help individuals achieve integrated, spiritual growth and holiness of life.

*We Request Your Feedback*

The Sacred Story Institute welcomes feedback on all our publications. Contact us via email or letter. Give us ideas, suggestions and inspirations for how to make better resources for Catholics and Christians of all ages and walks of life.

admin-team@sacredstory.net
Sacred Story Institute & Sacred Story Press
1401 E. Jefferson Suite 405
Seattle, Washington, 98122

# ENDNOTES

[i] **Kindergarten responses given orally to teacher:**

**HAPPY**

"Jesus, you helped me get better when I was sick for lots of days."

**SAD**

"When the fire burned the trees"


**Grade One:**

**HAPPY**

"I felt Jesus' hand on my back"

**SAD**

"I heard someone say that my dad was ill, because he was sick"


**Grade Two**

**HAPPY**

"When I had Thanksgiving at home"

**SAD**

"When Johnny's brother got hurt"


**Grade Three**

**HAPPY:**

"When people forgive me"

**SAD:**

"When I feel lonely"


**Grade Four**

**HAPPY**

"Family visiting time"

**SAD**

"When I don't get along with my sister"


**Grade Five**

**CONSOLATION**

"The beauty of the trees outside the window:

**DESOLATION**

"When Sara's dad got hurt in the war"

### Grade Six

**CONSOLATION**

"I felt joy from the music as Mass this morning"

**DESOLATION**

"The violence in the world"

### Grade Seven

**CONSOLATIONS:**
 "My mom helped me with my homework"

**DESOLATION:**
 "My friend got sick and had to go home:

### Grade Eight

**CONSOLATION**

"Donating my hair to *Locks of Love*"

**DESOLATION**

"When I fought with my parents"

Made in the USA
Las Vegas, NV
02 February 2023